From Goddess to Mortal
The True-Life Story of a Former Royal Kumari

FROM GODDESS TO MORTAL

The True-Life Story of a Former Royal Kumari

By
Rashmila Shakya

As Told to
Scott Berry

Vajra Books
www.vajrabooks.com.np

Published & Distributed by
Vajra Books
Jyatha, Thamel, P.O. Box 21779, Kathmandu, Nepal
Tel.: 977-1-4220562, Fax: 977-1-4246536
e-mail: bidur_la@mos.com.np
www.vajrabooks.com.np

© 2005 Rashmila Shakya and Scott Berry. All rights reserved. No part of this book may be reproduced in any form or by any means, electronic or mechanical, including photography, recording, or by any information storage or retrieval system or technologies now known or later developed, without permission in writing from the publisher.

Unless otherwise credited, all photos are either by Scott Berry or from Rashmila's family album.

Fifth Edition 2013

ISBN 978-9937-623-06-3

Printed in Nepal

Dedication

This book is respectfully dedicated to my two families: the family of Jujubhai Shakya of Kumari Che, who raised me as a goddess, and my original family, who taught me how to relate to the world as a human being.

It was late at night, and the old brick palace in the centre of Kathmandu with its many courtyards, its many fine carved wooden windows and its pagoda towers, was dark. The courtiers, the retainers and the king's wives had gone to bed, and only the sleepy guards still patrolled. In one room, however, there was a dim light, and two figures could be seen huddling over a board and throwing dice.

One was an unusually beautiful young woman, yet even the most casual of observers would notice that she was not only far too beautiful to be an ordinary mortal, but that she had an intense and penetrating third eye in the centre of her forehead. That she also had ten arms was less obvious, since she had a way of hiding 8 of them when they were not in use. She wore large golden earrings and golden tiara, and an aura glowed faintly around her head.

The other figure was that of the king. One might have expected him to be dressed informally at this time of night, but in fact he was in full royal regalia with his crown, peacock feather and jewels.

As they threw the dice, they spoke in undertones, and though the king's manner was respectful, there was between them the easy familiarity of a couple of long acquaintance.

"What to do about these restless six Pradhans of Lalitpur? And that Ghorkha Raja who threatens to swallow up every kingdom in his path?" asked the king, looking hopefully at the young woman for an answer.

"As to the first," she paused to throw the dice, and looked pleased with the result, "they pose little enough threat, and they should be handled with compassion so as not to alienate the people. But as to the latter ..."

There was no chance for her to finish, for at that point there was a disturbance, and the queen in night dress, followed by several armed attendants, bustled her way into the room.

"So this is how I find you. Discussing matters of state indeed! And with such a beautiful young woman!"

"But, my dear ..." the king began hopelessly.

"Can't trust you out of my sight for a moment!"

"Enough of this!" said the young woman, her voice full of authority, and indeed quite frightening as she drew herself up and spread her ten arms like wings. Eight of her ten hands held one of the attributes of her power. From her hips hung a belt of severed male heads, and she was now surrounded by an aura of flame. Three more lovely but frightening faces had appeared, one above the first, the other two on either side. Both the king and queen drew back in awe, while the retainers dropped their weapons, dumbstruck. "That you would think such a thing of me! I'll not put up with such human frailties as jealousy. You have seen the last of me."

"But how can I govern my kingdom without you?" pleaded the king.

"You cannot. Your reign will be short, and the end of your dynasty is near at hand." And with that, the goddess—for the queen in her jealousy had failed to recognise the goddess Taleju herself, wrathful aspect of Durga and patroness to the kings of Nepal—disappeared.

"Now look what you have done with your snooping and your jealousy!" said the king.

"How was I to know?"

"You could have simply minded your own business and let me mind mine!"

So dependant had the king grown on the advice of the goddess that he despaired of being able to govern his kingdom without her, so all through the next day he made offerings and kept the

Brahmins busy at the huge, three-storied pagoda where only he and the goddess's priests were allowed.

Eventually his prayers were answered, or at least partially, for that night the goddess appeared to him again in a dream.

"If you wish to see me again, choose a young virgin girl of the Shakya caste, beautiful and unblemished, with the 32 signs of perfection. Worship her as you would worship me. In her I will appear to you. But never will I forget the insult I have suffered."

And so, after consulting his priests, the king did her bidding. A four year-old girl of the Newar Shakya caste was found who met all the criteria. She was taken to the Taleju temple and installed as the living embodiment of the goddess. She was worshipped by the king and adored by the populace at festivals. A little later a small but ornate palace and temple where she could live was built for her just across from the palace. Once a year, during the great Indra Jatra festival, the king went to her temple to receive her blessings in the form of a tika, a red mark on his forehead.

Known as Kumari, the virgin goddess, or as Dyah Meiju to her own Newari people, as soon as she began to approach the age of womanhood she was replaced by a similar girl in order to assure that she would always be pure and unblemished and would never grow old. And so it continued throughout a change of dynasty, several centuries and many kings.

1

"Dyah Meiju, I have to talk to you." It was Pramila, the most serious of my sisters, almost four years my senior. I was playing on a swing that had been rigged in one of the back rooms of my temple, surrounded by deferential playmates of my own age and did not feel like being disturbed. Pramila had been coming to see me less and less recently as she worked up to her important School Leaving Certificate exam, and at any rate an intense and studious 16 year-old has little in common with a carefree 12-year-old. I did not feel particularly close to her and could not understand why she looked so insistent. As I often did when I was unsure how to react to her, I ignored her, and kept swinging.

"Dyah Meiju, please." Even my big sister, of course, had to address me as "goddess", and await my pleasure.

"Oh, all right. What is it?"

"Alone?"

Taking care to show my reluctance, I left the swing and walked over to her. After bowing and touching my feet, which were clad as always in red socks, she whispered to me, "In a week, you will be coming home. A new Kumari has already been chosen."

Though it was the first anyone had mentioned it aloud, the news did not come as a surprise. My whole family, that is the people who took care of me in the little palace and temple in the centre of Kathmandu where I lived, had been acting a little strangely, especially Taba, or "father's elder brother", as I called the gentle middle aged man whom I really thought of as my father. Now it all became clear.

"*Thaha chha,*" I replied as off-handedly as I could in Nepali, "I know," and skipped back to my swing, leaving my sister standing alone, as I so often had in the past. As the girl who had taken my place on the swing in my absence got down in deference to the 12-year-old in red (as was only right), I felt little emotion. In fact, I was becoming a little curious about what another life would be like, and I had always known that the one I was leading could not last forever. Little did I suspect, however, how totally my life would change, for the past 8 years had done almost nothing to prepare me for the hurly-burly of life in a big family where everyone pulled their weight and no one was indulged.

That unusual life which had shaped me into the adolescent I was had started with a visit to the royal palace to meet the king, at a time when I had been young enough not even to remember.

* * * *

I must have known something was happening that day. After all, even a four-year-old should be aware of being taken to the royal palace and being introduced to the king. Unfortunately, I have no memory at all of this except that I had a new dress for the occasion. It was white with red stripes and too big for me. In fact, it was the only time I ever wore it, because for the next eight years I was to wear only red. Pramila, who was seven at the time, inherited it.

I was taken to see the king because I had been chosen, all unknown to myself, to be the next Royal Kumari, or living virgin goddess, emanation of the fierce and powerful goddess Taleju Bhawani. For more or less the next eight years, I would live in my own palace/temple, be venerated as the human form of the goddess, be revered by crowds at our biggest festivals, be worshipped by the king himself, and be gaped at by foreign tourists. But at the time, all this meant very little to me, and it is not until a year or two later that I have any real remembrances of my life as Kumari.

The institution of Royal Kumari is a very old one in the Kathmandu valley. No one knows really how old it is. Some say it goes back to the 13th century, but this was nearly two hundred years before the arrival of the goddess Taleju herself. In the story told above, the king is usually Jayaprakesh Malla, who ruled Kathmandu from 1734 to 1768 AD, but sometimes it is Trailokya Malla who ruled the entire valley from Bhaktapur, near the eastern edge of the valley, between 1559 and 1615 AD. Since Jayaprakesh Malla was the last Malla king to rule Kathmandu before the Shah conquest, and there were also Royal Kumaris in the other two kingdoms of Patan and Bhaktapur, it is more likely to have been his ancestor.

But in actual fact, no one knows the historical origin of Kumari. The story I have told is only one of many, but it is the one I knew when I was Kumari. What all the tales have in common is that the goddess used to visit the king and advise him on how to run his kingdom. Somehow she was offended—in some versions by the queen, in others by a princess, and in yet others by the king himself, who looked at her in an improper way—and agreed to appear to him in future only in the form of a virgin girl of the Shakya caste. A date we can be more certain about is the construction of the present Kumari Che,[1] as we call the Kumari Palace in our Newari tongue, since the recently installed plaque there says it was built in 1757, 11 years before the fall of King Jayaprakesh Malla.

---

[1] *Che* is the Newari word for house. It is pronounced with a slight nasilised sound at the end, and might be more correctly, if rather awkwardly, written *che(n)*. The same building is also called Kumari Ghar and Kumari Chowk.

A girl can continue as Kumari only until roughly the age of puberty, and as my predecessor had reached the age of 12, her caretaker—who was soon to become mine—had decided that it was time to choose a new goddess. You might read in guidebooks or articles that the royal Kumari is disqualified the first time she sheds blood: a cut, bleeding from the loss of a tooth or first menstruation are the usual reasons given. But in fact, it is much simpler. Before any of these things happen, Kumari's caretaker goes around to Newari families of the Shakya caste who live inside the old city of Kathmandu and who have girls of the right age, looking for new candidates.

We Newars are the ancient people of the valley with our own language and culture. Some of us are Buddhist and some are Hindu, and we are tolerant enough that many of us participate in both Hindu and Buddhist festivals and we share our temples. In some ways I was to become the most prominent symbol of this tolerance. The Shakyas are Buddhist (in fact we believe that we descend from the same clan as Gautama Buddha, another of whose names was Shakya Muni, the "Sage of the Shakyas"), but I was to become a Hindu goddess.

The criteria for a potential Kumari are not nearly as strict as many people think. First of all, we have to be from a family of one of the Kathmandu *baha*. The word *"baha"* is a Newari version of the Sanskrit word "Vihar", and they are courtyards that were once Buddhist monasteries, but today are often family residences where Shakya families live. The Shakyas are usually described as "goldsmiths", and though many men follow that trade, it is actually a little more complicated than that. Among the Buddhist Newars, the two castes of Shakya and Bajracharya are considered to be the descendents of those who were once monks. Though only the Bajracharyas are now allowed to function as family Buddhist priests, both Shakya and Bajracharya boys undergo a ceremony called *bare chuegu* in which they become monks for four days and officially become members of a *baha*.

In addition to our fathers being members of one of the Kathmandu *baha*, there must not have been any inter-caste marriages in our ancestry. The girl herself must be around 3-5 years of age and must not have any scars or other marks on her body. Another condition is that she must not have been through either of two mock marriage ceremonies we have for little girls. In one, called *ihi*, which we usually do between the ages of 4 and 10, we are symbolically married to a fruit called a bel fruit. It is a growing up, or rite of passage ceremony, and afterwards we are expected to behave in a more mature manner. In the other, *bahrah*, a pre-menstrual ceremony usually done when we are between 10 and 15, but sometimes much younger, we are kept in a dark room with no males (but plenty of girlfriends and female relatives) allowed inside for 12 days, then symbolically married to the sun. These "marriages" are considered so important that a girl who has gone through either of them is no longer considered to be completely virgin, and so is ineligible to become Kumari, the Virgin Goddess.

At first the caretaker found four suitable girls: me, my sister Samjhana who is a year younger, and two others. I was not a particularly remarkable child except that I was extremely placid, and perhaps a little over-generous. As a baby, I had been thin, weak and very dark, but I am told that I was quiet and contented, and that except when I was wet, I never cried. At the age of three, when I started attending Miniland Kindergarten, if my friends would ask me, I would give them my lunch. Even if they just took it, I didn't complain. Soon my parents realised that I was coming home hungry, and they had to go and ask the teacher to make sure I ate my lunch instead of giving it away. Some of my relatives thought my generosity and passive nature might indicate that there was something unusual about me.

But there must have been something of the dreamer in me as well, for I had a habit of wandering off and getting lost during games of hide-and-seek in our big communal courtyard. This happened at least twice, much to the consternation of my older sisters who were in charge of me. Once I was found with a stranger at the nearest cross-roads, happily eating a chocolate.

The guidebooks, and some articles, will sometimes tell you that prospective Kumaris are subjected to a rigorous physical examination to determine if we are in possession of the *battis lagchan*, or the 32 bodily perfections. In fact, if you look over the list, you find a rather improbable little girl described (what four-year-old could have the body of a banyan tree and the chest of a lion and the voice of a duck?), and actually, these "32 perfections" all come from our horoscopes. Most important, the horoscope of the girl who is chosen also has to have no conflict with that of the king.

There *is* a physical examination, conducted by the wife of the Mul Purohit (the Royal Priest) and her daughter, but according to my mother, who was also present, it was not particularly rigorous or intimate. I kept my underclothes on, and was looked over mainly to see if I was cross-eyed, had any birthmarks or scratches, or had lost any of my teeth. I do not remember it at all, and only know about it from my mother.

If none of us had qualified, the caretaker would have gone on to find four more girls. But of the four, I turned out to have the ideal horoscope, so the search never had to go any further. My younger sister Samjhana was generally thought to be more attractive, but it was March or April, two of the hottest months in Kathmandu, and she had a heat rash which disqualified her. My mother, as well, sensibly hoped that the choice would fall on Samjhana, but for the practical reason that she had not yet started her schooling, whereas my fledgling educational career at Miniland Kindergarten would be interrupted. Samjhana did not find out until she was five or six that she had also been considered, and the other two girls may never have learned.

My family was now given a week to prepare for the loss of a daughter. I have been told that, honoured as he was, my father was not too happy about me leaving home at the tender age of four, though the caretaker's wife was his sister, the Kumari Che is only a few hundred metres from our 200 year old house in the oldest part of southern Kathmandu and he would be able to visit whenever he wanted. My mother, who had now given birth to four daughters and was wondering if she would ever have a son, was apparently less unwilling.

It was during the following week that I got my new dress, was made to keep strictly to the diet that everyone of the Shakya caste should follow (no chicken, chicken eggs or pork, with the addition in my case of no "rough" food, which in practice meant no snacks with friends) and was introduced to King Birendra Bir Bikram Shah Dev, still an absolute monarch at the time, at the Narayanhiti palace. Also during that week I was taken to what would be my new home, across from the old royal palace in Durbar Square, on several occasions, so that I would not be completely unfamiliar with it. I am not sure if the twelve-year-old Kumari whom I would be replacing knew or cared who her visitor was.

On the day of my formal installation, I was taken first to the huge pagoda temple of Taleju, the goddess whose emanation I was to become, for a puja. Whatever rites took place at this time, I have no remembrance of them. Nor do I remember the journey of a hundred metres or so to the Kumari Che, the streets crowded with people watching me, although you would have thought such an experience would have made a strong impression. At my new house I was dressed for the first time in red, and my new caretaker, in the presence of my predecessor, presented me with what might be called my badge of office, a gold necklace encrusted with gems of 9 colours with the figure of a *naga*, or snake, on it. You can see it on all the postcards of Kumari at festivals. This was the most powerful of my ornaments, and when I was older I would notice a change come over me whenever I wore it. The old Kumari would now go home in full Kumari regalia except for the naga, and for the next four days would still be revered as a goddess.

But I am only aware of all this now because other people have told me, and because eight years later, in 1991, I was the 12-year-old who was leaving. My real memories only begin about a year later, but it was not until I was about 8 or 9 that I became fully aware of who, and what, I was.

2

The Living Goddess Kumari is a Supreme Goddess .... and She does not undergo any lessons or teaching. She also does not have any playmates. Her caretakers keep a watch on her day and night.

From, Siddhi B. Ranjitkar:
Kumari, the Virgin Goddess

Very little light comes in through the traditional, carved wooden windows of my bedroom in the morning. They face in towards the courtyard, so there is little sound either, even though the square outside by this time is full of the honking of early morning rickshaws, the swish of the long brooms of the sweepers, the bells of the temples and the chanting of priests. I hear only the vaguest echoes of all this, as I see only the palest reminder of the sun. But no one ever has to wake me up. I look forward to opening my eyes every morning and seeing all my dolls looking at me, for I have arranged them around my bed the night before.

Once I have greeted them, I make the long trip to my own bathroom, around a corner, up the steep stairs to the next floor, and down a passageway, where I find my red towel and red toothbrush. Already others are stirring, and I know that when I get back to my room Fufu, or "father's sister" (whom I think of as my mother, even though she really is my father's sister), or possibly one of her daughters Durga or Sita (usually Sita) will be there to help me dress and put up my hair. Dressing is something I can do well enough by myself as long as it is not a festival day, but I enjoy having my hair combed out and put up, even though it is pulled so tight that sometimes it hurts.

"Hold still, please Dyah Meiju," she warns as she pulls it up into a bun on the top of my head, and then puts a red ribbon around it. "Now for your *aajha*." She carefully applies kohl around my eyes, and then in two sweeping curves to above my ears. I will not be able to rub my eyes all day. With her right thumb she puts a red tika on my forehead between my eyes, and I am set up for the day.

By now it is breakfast time. I always enjoy breakfast because it is a meal I can share with others. Meals including cooked rice are considered special, so I must eat them alone on a raised platform in my own kitchen in the back of the palace. Since breakfast is only tea and deep-fried bread there is no restriction on where I have to be or whom I have to eat it with, and as a result it is an informal and enjoyable affair.

"Dyah Meiju, your teacher is here!" a woman's voice calls. That must mean it is 9 o'clock, for the teacher arrives from the school next door at that time. After finishing my tea, I go back to my room where he is waiting. The building is now astir with children getting ready to go to school.

"Dyah Meiju, the priest from the Taleju Temple has arrived," comes another voice. "It is time for *Nitya* Puja." This is always done around 9 am, but since the exact time is not important, sometimes—if the priest is late—my lesson can begin before the puja.

"Which one?" I call out.

"The young one." The one who gets on my nerves. The Acahju, or chief priest, is a dignified, elderly man who commands respect by his manner, so that there is no question of any nonsense with him. But the younger, stouter, priest, seems always to be irritated about something, and frequently loses his temper with everyone, except me of course.

I see one of my playmates hurrying by in her school uniform, and point to the stairway where the priest will leave his puja bag after taking out the items he will need. She smiles back in understanding. Not only does she have to do whatever I want her to do, but this is one of our favourite, often repeated, games. As soon as the priest is in the puja room with me, she will hide his bag.

I go into the room called the Singhasan, the one with the golden window looking out onto the street, and sit on my golden throne with seven nagas protecting me while the priest sits on the floor offering red powder, rice and flowers to my feet, and lighting small lamps, as he worships the human embodiment of the goddess Taleju for about fifteen minutes. This puja also includes the indistinct chanting of secret *mantras* and the performance of secret *mudras*, or hand gestures. Since not even I am allowed to know these, he covers his hands while performing the gestures. He will not offer me a tika, for he is allowed only to touch my feet. Only the women of the family are allowed to give me tika. Though the same ceremony is repeated every morning, and I no longer pay attention, I never get bored or fidgety, but simply sit there in my stony-faced way. I know that I am a goddess, that this is the way a goddess is treated and this is the way she behaves.

I know that I probably won't start my lesson now, for this is the time when worshippers usually come, and for the past week the same woman and her son have been here. The boy is about 6 or 7 years old, perhaps 2 or 3 years younger than I am, but he has still not begun to speak, and his mother has brought him every day in the hopes that I will be able to cure him. Most of my devotees have children with problems, particularly illnesses, so that I know I am important to children. I also have no doubt that I will be able to help him. Of course the mother does not ask me directly for what she wants, nor do I speak directly to her. Instead I remain seated on my golden throne while she pours a small amount of water from her left hand over my feet into her right hand then drinks it. She repeats this, but this time offers the water to the boy who also drinks it. In the distance I hear with satisfaction the priest fuming and shouting about thieves and missing puja bags, but I force myself to concentrate on the task at hand, for it is my duty to try to help the boy to speak.

Since it is a weekday, I hope that there will be no more worshippers so that I can finally begin my lesson. The teacher has only been coming for the last year, and every day our lesson is interrupted in this way, but I have discovered that learning can be fun, and I want to catch up with my playmates, all of whom go to the Nawa Adahrsa School next door in Basantapur Square. "One more worshipper this morning, Dyah Meiju," says Taba, the man whom I regard as my father.

Actually I am ready for this one because the family of the supplicant has paid for everything necessary for a *chemma*, or forgiveness puja and Taba has made all the arrangements, having first asked me if there was anything I would particularly like. A pale and ill-looking young man comes into the room with his family and looks at me hopefully. I know that I will be able to cure him if I want to, though since he is not a child, I am not particularly interested.

It seems he has unwittingly got himself into trouble with me. It is not the first time I have seen him, for he is a journalist who came to do a story about Kumari. It happens all the time and I always enjoy these visits because I get to hear yet again the stories about the Goddess Taleju and King Jayaprakesh Malla, or of Prithvi Narayan Shah dreaming of Kumari just before he conquered the Kathmandu valley. It is not that this young man actually wrote anything bad or untrue, but when the article appeared, his picture was inset above mine. Although I was entirely unaware of this, it was apparently enough of an insult to Taleju Bhawani as personified in me, that the poor man began vomiting blood. This puja is to ask my forgiveness so that he will be cured. No wonder he looks anxious. If I do not accept his puja, I can make things even worse for him. I have heard the story of an elderly priest who offered water to my predecessor, who stared hard at him before condescending to drink it. He died on the way home.

I am first offered chocolates and the red toy car I had requested. More importantly I am offered *sagun*, which consists of a boiled egg and a dried fish which are placed in my left hand, and a silver tumbler of *raksi*, the strong distilled spirit of the valley, which I hold in my right. Each of these items I touch to my lips to show that I accept the offering, to the visible relief of the young journalist. The *raksi* burns my lips pleasantly.

There was no question of my not accepting his puja. Though children are the only ones I really care about, I have no hostile feeling towards anyone, not even the irritable priest whom I enjoy tormenting, and am happy enough for him to be cured.

At last my long-delayed lesson can begin, though by now it is nearly 10 o'clock, the time when my teacher always leaves. I go back to my bedroom and sit opposite him on the floor with a small table between us. He is a very old man, tall and thin with thick, black-rimmed glasses that seem almost an extension of his black Nepali *topi*. Like the priest, he is dressed in the traditional Nepali *Daura Surwal*. He is not very energetic, or, it would seem, very interested in the lesson. But in a way I am lucky to have him at all, for there is a belief that it can serve no purpose to attempt to teach a goddess, who by definition already knows everything. There is an even more discouraging legend that anyone who tries to teach a Kumari will die. But he does not seem afraid. In fact he hardly seems conscious.

"Not much time," he grumbles in Nepali in his thin, wheezy voice. My families (both of them) speak to me in our Newari language of the Kathmandu valley. Since I had started Kindergarten before becoming Kumari I had made a start in Nepali, as all school children do. The old man is a Nepali teacher, and this cannot help but be useful to me, but he is expected to teach me other subjects like English and Mathematics as well. "Would Dyah Meiju be so good as to multiply 17 times 14?" he asks.

"Two hundred and thirty-eight," I answer mechanically, hoping he will come up with something a little more interesting. His mathematics lessons consist of making me memorise the multiplication tables up to 22. My eldest sister Pramila, who visits me occasionally, but not often enough that I feel really close to her, says he should be giving me word problems, whatever they are.

"Yes, well that's good," he mumbles, sounding as if he is about to fall asleep. "Now, would Dyah Meiju kindly copy out these English words?"

I open my notebook and copy out a few words, taking special care to reproduce them exactly in all their elegance, for the letters are beautiful and exotic to me. "What do they mean?" I ask. He looks blank. "Are they really words? What do they sound like?"

"Time enough for that when Dyah Meiju has learned how to copy them. Mustn't try to run before we can walk." Even at nine years old, I suspect that he will not tell me because he just does not know.

Outside, in the distance, a school bell rings. "Time to go," he mutters struggling to his feet and forgetting to give me any homework. It hardly matters, for we will probably be interrupted again tomorrow.

My duties, such as they are, have finished for the day, and I go in search of playmates. The house is large, made up of many long narrow rooms and passages, much larger than the house where I spent my first three years, though I have no real memories of that. There are many children here, for Taba has two married sons and plenty of nieces and nephews. Enough of them are my own age that it should not be difficult to find someone to play with, and in fact until a year or two ago it never was. But in recent years they are all at the Nawa Adahrsa School, the one my teacher comes from.

Going from one long room to another, then down several passageways, and finding no one but my "big brothers" Gautam Dai and Mahendra Dai,[1] their wives and sisters, all of whom are much too old to play with, I decide to play with my dolls. I have a large collection. Some are dolls that have been bought in stores and have been offered to me by grateful devotees whose children I have cured, others are rag-dolls I make from bits of red cloth and discard when I am finished with them.

What should I do? Perhaps make a sari or a dress for one of them, or should I set them up in family groups? I decide on the latter and begin dragging them out of my room and setting them up in the side room that runs from the back to the Singhasan puja room, on the opposite side of the courtyard from the kitchens. Soon I have a big pile, and then I begin sorting them out so that some can be eating, others cooking, others still sewing and gossiping. Most are girls, blonde and pale-skinned, though I do give them red tikas to make them seem more familiar. Their eyes shut when I lay them down. Sometimes one of the girls has to pretend to be a father doll, but there are plenty of babies, including one which never leaves its basket, and a couple of rag dolls. I bring out my little stove that another worshipper has given me, and all its miniature pots and pans. Everything works, and I have even learned how to light the little coal stove. Taba and Fufu have not been happy about this, fearing that I might hurt myself, but seeing that I was careful, they have let me go ahead with it.

"The sun is in the right place. Perhaps Dyah Meiju would like to have her bath now." It is Sita, one of my "sisters" who usually helps me with my bath. Actually Dyah Meiju would rather play

---

[1] *Dai* is Nepali for elder brother.

with her dolls just now, but I know that at this time of year, if I don't have my bath when the sun is shining in the window, it will be cold and unpleasant, so I reluctantly leave my dolls and follow Sita to my bathroom. The winter sun streams in the window which overlooks the back courtyard with its quacking ducks. No one but the family has access to this courtyard. It wouldn't do to have Kumari drying herself in the sun where she can be seen by just anyone.

The water in the bucket has been heated, and it feels pleasant as it is poured over me. I could manage my bath by myself, but no one has ever suggested this, and besides, I will need help with my hair and eye make-up when it is finished. It feels good afterwards to stand in the sun wrapped in my red towel until it is time to get dressed and go to lunch. This time, since I will be eating rice, I go and sit on my solitary platform in my own kitchen, while Fufu places a tray of *dal-bhat-tarkari* in front of me. This consists of hot cooked rice, potato curry, a mixed vegetable curry, and (what my eyes have searched for first) a spicy pickle made from tomatoes. "I'm glad to see that there is tomato *achar* today," I say a trifle haughtily and self-righteously.

"Oh yes, Dyah Meiju has no need to worry."

Last week I was served a lunch with no tomato achar, and refused to eat it until Fufu had gone out, bought tomatoes, and cooked them up into *achar*. I simply sat there until two o'clock when I finally got what I wanted. Dyah Meiju always gets what she wants.

The long afternoon stretches before me. My playmates are still in school, and I drift first to the front windows where I look out onto Durbar Square and the people passing by. There are rickshaw drivers hoping to get a foreign tourist, ragged, bare-legged porters smoking a cigarette after carrying a heavy load, another staggering under the weight of a refrigerator strapped to his forehead. A Newari farmer carries vegetables in two baskets suspended from a carrying pole across his shoulders. Country women in colourful red saris are sitting on the steep steps of the Narayan Temple gossiping, while the occasional taxi blasts on its horn. Children my own age run around, some in blue or maroon school uniforms, others in rags. A little drama unfolds as a man on a motorbike almost knocks a man off a bicycle, but it all ends in smiles and laughter. A man with a tie and a briefcase, making his Nepali topi look incongruous, hurries across the space in front of my temple like his life depended on it. What can be so important? A woman I recognise is trying to sell little bags and necklaces to the groups of foreigners coming in my direction, and is using her little boy to get their sympathy.

My view is limited since I am not supposed to stick my head right out, but though I can see only the white Ghadi Bhaitak part of the Palace, where the King and his family wait for me on the first day of Indra Jatra, and three temples, it is really the people who interest me. Some are richer than me, most are not nearly so well off, but they all have something I do not have: they can all go where they want. I wonder, with no way at all of solving the puzzle, whether the ragged urchins playing tag have more interesting lives than mine. I try to imagine myself in their place, but it is just too hard.

I shrink back a little from the window so the foreigners will not be able to see me. In a few minutes, after the trinket lady finishes with them, I will probably have to show myself to them from the window in the back. My eyes go up to the window of another temple across the square where I see the lord Shiva with his arm around his wife Parvati. Like me they are looking out of a window and down at the square, but they are even more trapped, for as wooden images they cannot even leave their window. Then I hear one of the women of the house call, "Dyah Meiju, some foreign visitors."

It is not an order, for no one orders a goddess around, but I understand that because they will leave an offering on a small pillar in the courtyard, I have a duty to show myself at the window, just as I understand that I have a duty not to smile when I am there. Sometimes it is a bother, if I am playing with my dolls or dancing with the other children, but just now I don't mind. If I am not doing anything else and I like the looks of them, I might appear even if they have not left an offering.

Going back through the room where my dolls are still as I left them, I put on my serious Kumari face and step to the window. Sometimes the foreigners applaud, some of them do Namaste, and some just stand and stare. Sometimes I stay longer than others, depending on how curious I am. Where are they from, I wonder? Why are the women dressed so strangely? Is their hair that way naturally? Most of them, men and women, have cameras around their necks, but I know that if they point them at me I should step back. I wonder what country they are from, and wish I could just shout down and ask their Nepali guide. What is that country of theirs like? Would my teacher know if I asked him? Will I ever visit it? And what do they make of me? Don't they have goddesses in their own land? Wouldn't it be nice if I could just ask them whatever I wanted? Of all of them, the ones I like most are the ones I am told come from a country called Japan. They always applaud when I come to the window, and something in the way they look at me makes me think they understand me.

A little hesitantly, and without any real hope, I look down to one corner of the courtyard. No, as I expected they are not there. It has been about two years since I have seen them, two foreign girls a little older than me, dressed like Nepali girls in grubby *salwar khameez*. For a long time they came every day, sitting and looking up at me and smiling when I appeared for the tourists. Then one day when no one else was around, I called down to them that I had a ball, and why didn't we play? Of course they could not actually come in since they were not Hindu, but Taba, Gautam and Mahendra decided they could come to the bottom of the steps while I stood at the top and we could throw the ball back and forth. Sometimes they threw me sweets, and at others I would throw down some of my offerings. We could even talk since they spoke some Nepali.

But that was years ago. Just who they were or where they were from I never learned. Kids don't talk about things like that when they are playing ball and eating sweets. Will they ever come back?

Having seen enough of the palace square for the moment, once the foreigners have gone I wander into the kitchen used by my guardians. This is separate from my own, for everything of mine is used only by me, and food can only be prepared for me in my own special kitchen. The reason I like the family kitchen is because the window looks right out on to Nawa Adharsa School at right angles, and I am almost close enough to touch the children in the classrooms. I can almost tell what subject they are studying from what they are writing in their notebooks. Of course not everyone is writing intently. Some, especially the boys, are misbehaving, throwing things at one another, or annoying the girls. Occasionally I hear the rough voice of a teacher, a teacher more energetic than mine, bringing them to order. It looks like fun. In fact at the moment, it looks a lot better than standing around waiting for everybody else to finish school.

I wonder if I can get away with feeding the fish without Gautam Dai noticing. I know he says it is bad for them, but everyone likes to eat, so why not fish? Hoping that he is in the little shop that he runs next to Kumari Che, I sneak to the back of the house where he has a nice aquarium full of colourful fish, but just as I am reaching for the food, I see that he has noticed me and has followed me. He must have come back for lunch. "Now, Dyah Meiju," he says, gently taking the box of fish food from my hand. "The fish have already been fed today, and you know that you might kill them if you give them too much. Let's go check on the birds."

He also likes to keep pigeons, and there are a lot of ducks as well. Knowing that I can eat duck eggs, but not chicken eggs, my devotees often offer baby ducks to be raised in one of the back rooms of the Kumari Che around the small back courtyard. I like the baby ducks, but lose interest in them as they grow up. For one thing, they smell bad. For another, one of my 32 perfections is to have a voice "as soft and clear as a duck's." Not very flattering. But there happens to be a fat puppy waddling around which I pick up and cuddle, somewhat to Gautam's consternation.

But I now hear the noise of children returning, and hurry up to the long, narrow rooms occupied by the family on the first floor to listen to the news of my playmates' day at school. They look a little uncomfortable as I join them, for when we are together, the word of the girl in red is law. "Go ahead," I tell them after they have all touched my feet. "Don't stop. I want to hear about your school." Normally I just sit and listen, since I have nothing to contribute, as they talk about their lessons, complain about the naughty boys, and go on about who is friends with whom. I hear that a girl named Dilmaya got top marks on the English test, but a boy named Bikas was jealous, and he pulled her hair, so the teacher made him stand in the corner for the rest of the day. It is all a world away from mine, though the school is so close by. No one else seems to be learning the times tables up to 22. Maybe only goddesses do that. One day I will go to school, I'm sure, but just now it is very hard to imagine. Besides, when they talk about the short tempers of their teachers, sometimes I have my doubts.

Two girls, a little older than my playmates, come and join the group, though first they bow and touch my feet. My big sisters. Thin and rather intense, Pramila is already beginning to look like a young woman, and to act like one as well. Surmila, year older than I am, is a lot more jolly and carefree. I ignore them. It is not that I don't like them, but I have never really figured out how to act with them. The children, grandchildren, neices and nephews of the caretaker are kids I see all the time. We know how to behave with one another. But my sisters, whom I only see perhaps once a week or even less, are a mystery to me. Should they treat me with the deference and respect other outsiders do, or should we act like I have seen other sisters acting?

"Come sit with us, Dyah Meiju," suggests Surmila, the bolder of the two. I run away to my dolls.

The other children never come to play with me, but have to wait for me to come to them. Just now I want to be alone, so I take my little stove and go to my own kitchen where it is safe to light it, since I feel like making some snacks for my dolls. As the newspaper and wood chips light the charcoal and the stove heats up, I put on the tiny kettle and cut up a potato. This is something else that my guardians were not happy with at first, worrying that I might cut myself, but seeing that I was skilful enough not to do myself any harm, they gave in and let me have my own way. Eventually I wind up with something that is supposed to be tea and fried potatoes, which I serve to my dolls. It would be nice sometime to do this for real people, and to see them actually eat and hear them say what a clever cook I am, but of course I am not allowed to do anything for anyone else. After my dolls have finished with them, I usually give their snacks to the family, but am not sure what they do with them.

"Dyah Meiju, foreigners." I am busy feeding my dolls, and do not want to go, but I know it is my duty. It is no problem not smiling this time. I positively glower.

Afterwards I interrupt two of my playmates from a game of *karom* in one of the back rooms, and have them come and help me feed my dolls. Recently I have been spending a lot of time with my dolls, and I know that my playmates are bored with them, but what is that to me? After a few minutes, they grow restless. "Would not Dyah Tata perhaps like to join in our *karom* game?" one suggests shyly. Only my playmates in the temple address me as "goddess sister". I am not in the mood for flipping disks of wood around a board and trying to get them into the holes in the corners, and I can force them to do whatever I want, but it is more pleasant playing with happy people, so I give in with the air of someone doing them a big favour.

"Tea time." My dolls have had their tea, and now it is my turn: *roti* or maybe fried potatoes and a sweet. Since cooked rice is not involved, I do not have to have my tea on my platform, and so I can sit around and talk with my playmates or whomever else I want to talk with.

After tea I find my mother waiting in the back room. Much more important as far as I am concerned, she has brought my little brother Sarbagya with her. He is now a fat toddler about two and a half years old, and before my mother even has time to touch my feet, I grab him and spin him around. He is my favourite of the family, by a long way, and while he is here I will not let go of him.

At last my mother, who is not much taller than I am, manages to get under him to touch my feet. Of course in a normal Newari family, a child bows down to touch his or her parents' feet, and this act of homage paid to me is something that makes it difficult for me to think of her as my mother. She then confuses me even more by ceasing to treat me as a goddess and chatting about my health (I am always fine) and about how my sisters are doing in school. Pramila is doing brilliantly as always, and is making everyone proud as the others try hard to emulate her. As with my sisters, I am not sure how to behave. The family always makes me feel terribly shy. Like my sisters, she wants me to sit beside her, and since she has brought my brother, I acquiesce, keeping him on my lap.

I enjoy her visits more since he was born. I used to be so shy with her that I found it easiest to just ignore her, though even as a small child I could see that I hurt her. For some reason, even when she was pregnant with my brother, I began to feel closer to her (though this did not happen when she was pregnant with my youngest sister Sunila just a year before) and once he was born we were both just crazy over him. For her it came as a tremendous relief after five girls to finally have a boy, and since the previous Kumari's mother had also had a son while she was in office, I got a lot of the credit.

Dinner, like lunch, is a solitary affair, but not particularly lonely. From my platform as I eat my *dal-bhat-tarkari* (and of course my tomato *achar*) I can not only hear the members of my family, my guardian family that is, chatting away and joking about events of the day, but I can see some of them as well. Their dining room is right next to mine, and I can even join in the conversation if I want.

After dinner I feel like company, but my playmates are doing their homework. I could make them form a little band and sing for me so I could dance, the way the star does in the Hindi and Nepali movies, but not wanting to chance the unhappy looks I get from both them and their parents when they cannot refuse, I go upstairs to where there is a large, glass-covered portrait of King Mahendra, King Birendra's father and predecessor. I use this as a mirror, and dance some of the numbers I have seen in Hindi and Nepali movies, imagining myself as the heroine. When I get bored with this I return to my dolls. They are still arranged in the long room opposite the kitchens, so I gather them all up in two or three trips and take them to my room. They will be my company when I curl up between my red sheets, and I arrange them so that whenever I wake up I will find them looking at me.

Everyone is tired now, and before bed-time we usually gather in the long first floor sitting room overlooking the courtyard to watch television. This is something new in our country, and everyone is quite fascinated by the pictures on the small screen. As the goddess, I get to sit right in front of the screen so that no one can block my view. I am so amazed that I hardly ever remember what I have seen except the dancers in the films. If I were not a goddess, sometimes I think I would like to be a dancer.

Before I go to bed I go to my bathroom and wash off my eye make-up. Then one of my "sisters" comes to take down my hair and help me out of my red dress and into my red pyjamas. I am not really supposed to add any personal touches to my room, but she overlooks the dolls.

It has been a day much like any other, though there are occasional variations. On the 10th day of some of the Nepali months one of a group of five priests called the Pancha Buddha perform a special puja with me called *Dasami* Puja. These are five priests of the Bajracharya caste representing the "Five Buddhas" that are seen everywhere in the Kathmandu Valley: particularly painted over doorways and on stupas, large and small. Each of them has his own colour and, when on a stupa, each faces one of the cardinal points, except for Vairochana who is usually considered to be at the centre (though on some of the larger stupas, like Suwayambunath, he faces just south of east). One of their human representations comes every morning to Kumari Che for a puja in a special room called the Agan Kota, but the only one that involves me is *Dasami* Puja. I can never differentiate between them, and think of all of them as "Guruju".[1]

On a Saturday, a holiday for everyone else, I will be busier with worshippers—there might be twenty or more—and there will be no shortage of playmates since there is no school that day. I have little to do during the day, everyone looks up to me, and hardly anyone ever tells me what I can and can't do. But sometimes I am lonely, and of course I am always looking forward to those 13 occasions during the year when I get to go outside my temple.

---

[1] Books and articles always say that they are involved in the Kumari selection process, but as far as I know, this is not true.

From Goddess to Mortal

King Jayaprakesh Malla seemed to be behaving in a less and less rational manner all the time. The Valley of Kathmandu was surrounded by the forces of Prithvi Narayan Shah who had already taken the town of Kirtipur. Yet rather than defending his walled city, the king had ordered preparations to go ahead for the grandest public spectacle of the year, the festival of Indra Jatra. His soldiers, instead of preparing for battle, were all drunk in preparation for pulling the chariot of the virgin goddess Kumari.

And yet there may have been method in his madness. Every year, the little girl who embodied Taleju Bhawani blessed his rule by placing a tika on his forehead. It was believed by him, as well as by his people, that the tika would assure his successful reign for the upcoming year. And so, while it might be hopeless to battle the forces of the Ghorkha Raja, who after all had defeated even a British force sent against him, if the king could only get his tika on this day, he would be safe for another year.

For the goddess Taleju had not completely deserted him. But he could no longer rely on her to advise him, though he often needed her counsel. He wished he had heeded her about the six Pradhans of Lalitpur, for by humiliating them and making them beg in the streets he had so alienated the people that he had lost all influence there. She had predicted that his reign would be short, but how short? Perhaps she had changed her mind, just as she had changed her mind about never appearing to him again.

If he could only get his tika, he would be safe. Yet it was not to be. Among the enemies he had made by his erratic behaviour were the Brahmins of the city, who had let Prithvi Narayan Shah and his soldiers in one of the unguarded gates. The king had not yet reached Kumari's temple when he saw he was cut off by them, and he turned and fled to fight another day.

Prithvi Narayan, however, ignored him. Instead, believing as sincerely as Jayaprakesh Malla and everyone else that a tika from Kumari would insure a prosperous reign, he went straight to the temple of Kumari and presented himself respectfully before her. That day a king received his tika, but it was not Jayaprakesh Malla.

The new king ordered the festival to continue. It is even said that he pulled the chariot himself, and ever since then the kings of Nepal have been of the Shah dynasty.

3

It seems that there is always a festival somewhere in one of the cities or towns of our valley. During those years when I was Kumari, nine of them were particularly important for me, for these were the only occasions when I came out of my palace. On one of them in particular, Indra Jatra in the early autumn, I came out on four separate occasions, and this is one of the reasons that it was my favourite. Some of the shorter ones, when I went no further than Hanuman Dhoka—the old palace—or the gate of the Taleju Temple, were over in less time than it took me to dress for them, and they tend to be a little confused in my mind. But there was a certain excitement to all of them, for these were the only times when I got to see more than I could in the restricted view from my window.

During the monsoon in July or August, was one of the more disappointing ones, when the ancient image of Changu Narayan is carried from its hilltop temple in the north-east and I was brought out to greet it. It would take Fufu or one of my sisters, Durga or Sita, about an hour to dress me in the simpler of my festival dresses, the one brocaded with imitation gold thread, to put on my third eye, and my simpler *mokut* (head dress) made of cloth flowers, and of course my naga necklace which I only wore for special occasions. I am not sure at what age I first began to notice feeling different whenever the naga necklace was put on, but wearing it I suddenly felt myself to be in some way apart from and superior to the people around me, and I never felt like talking to anyone. Nor did I ever feel like smiling. It is not actually true that Kumari is forbidden to smile, but once she is dressed up with the naga necklace on, it would never occur to her.[1]

I did not even get in a palanquin for this one, but was simply carried in the arms of one of my brothers behind a couple of musicians. In my younger years, I found it was only Mahendra-Dai, my eldest brother who could carry me comfortably. Since sometimes some of my elder cousins would carry me as well, at some point I got fed up with their bungling efforts, and made them start practising in Kumari Che until they got it right.

As is sometimes the case, the actual image of Changu Narayan was not brought, but he was represented by a silver pot. A few women always seemed to want to touch my feet and do a brief puja to me. Otherwise, few people were aware of this little event, and I would be carried to the Taleju hardly being noticed, though a few surprised and curious worshippers and tourists would see me and tag along.

At the gate of the Taleju Temple was a military band dressed in the uniform of the 18th century, some musketeers in similar uniform and three men carrying silver pots around their necks. My only function was to observe the offerings being made to the pot in the centre representing the god. When this was finished, and it took no longer than ten or fifteen minutes, four ancient muskets fired a salute, the pot was whisked into the open gate of the Taleju, the military band marched back to the palace and I was carried back to my temple, having seen nothing more than the streets around Hanuman Dhoka. I always felt a little disappointed.

But the next few days would make up for it. First came Gai Jatra, a festival in which I took only the briefest part by offering a cow to a Brahmin the day before. I did not even come outside to

---

[1] I have to admit, however, that there is a photo of me when I was about five years old that I love, in which I was being carried and was grinning from ear to ear.

do this, but simply touched the rope that was tied to both the cow (in front of Kumari Che) and an upstairs window.

Yet while I took no more active part in the festival, I could watch from the front window. Gai Jatra, or the Cow Festival, is a day for people who have lost a family member during the year to remember the person and to put their grief behind them. The story behind the festival is that a son of King Jayaprakesh Malla (the same one who in some of the tales first worshipped Kumari) had died and that his queen was inconsolable. In order to make her realise that her grief was excessive, he ordered all of his subjects who had lost a family member during the year to parade through the streets, so the queen could see she was not alone; but he also asked his subjects to try and make her laugh. This is why people not only march through the streets, but boys and young men dress up as cows. They don't actually look very much like cows, but they are very entertaining. Even more entertaining were the adults, who were intentionally outrageous, some of them holding umbrellas with no cover, or wearing necklaces of chillies. I had to be a little careful when I went to the window, for although it was no problem for Nepalis to see me, foreigners were always trying to take my picture, and it is strictly forbidden to photograph Kumari's "private life" (that is, any time she is inside her temple). Yet they only needed to wait till the next day to have had as many chances as they wanted.

For another nice thing about Gai Jatra was that when it came I knew that one of my favourite festivals of the year was coming up the next day. Bahi Dyah Jatra did not have the sheer excitement of Indra Jatra, nor the solemnity of Dasain, but it was the longest distance I travelled on my palanquin. During the second half of the Buddhist holy month of Gunla, many of the *baha*, or courtyards centred around ancient temples, display their images and paintings, and the purpose of the procession is to take me to see them. During this procession, I got to visit six temples (or in later years, only four, since two of them were either undergoing renovation or had had their images stolen), but even more important, it was the time I got to see the most of the street life of the city, for unlike Indra Jatra when people lined the street waiting for me, on this occasion no one seemed to expect me except at the points where we stopped.

No one ever seemed to know exactly when the procession was going to start, not for any spiritual or astrological reasons, but simply because we had to wait for everyone to arrive, especially the band which came all the way from Bhaktapur. No one ever started to dress me or make me up until everyone arrived, for why should I have to wait for them? Though I was excited at the prospect before me, I was never restless or cross at the people who took so long to arrive. Looking back at my time as Kumari, I am sometimes amazed at how calm I could be.

When all was ready one of my "brothers" would carry me to the small palanquin which had been decorated just outside the gate of the Kumari Che. The waiting palanquin, its dome covered with red brocaded silk, always attracted a crowd of on-lookers, and there would be a hundred or more by the time I was carried out and placed in my seat, many of them clicking away with cameras and flashes, for now that I was outside, there were no restrictions on photographing me. Special friends or influential journalists were allowed right up to the palanquin for close-ups. And then I was hoisted on the shoulders of four strong men and we were off.

Generally during a palanquin procession, a Kumari not only does not smile, but seems to be gritting her teeth. There is, in fact, a reason for this. The men who carry the palanquin are all of different heights, which gives it a very strange movement. I always felt as if I could slide off at any moment, so it was very reassuring to have Gautam on one side and Mahendra on the other, holding my hands and keeping me steady.

I was whisked across Durbar Square to Pyaphel Tol, the street going north towards Chhetrapati, at a very brisk pace. Once in this street, things started to get interesting as women began to throw flowers and coins, touched their foreheads to the palanquin, and as irritated taxi drivers—wondering what the hold-up was—began honking their horns. We did not spend long on this street, but soon turned right into a narrower one called Kilagal as we neared our first stopping point, the vast, ancient courtyard of Itumbaha.

Although the people inside the *baha* were expecting me, the man making curries in a wok by the gate and the woman selling vegetables looked extremely surprised as the band of flutes and drums approached and a crowd gathered. Either Gautam Dai or Mahendra Dai would then pick me up and we would plunge into the waiting crowd of worshippers. Itumbaha was one of my favourite spots for a number of reasons. First, the rest of Taba's family lived there. These were the people I really regarded as my immediate family, and in fact they were all relatives by marriage. I would have thought of them as my cousins even if they had not been, and I used to look all around the buildings until I spotted them, and would even try to give a secret little wave. And then there were the crowds of children who seemed genuinely happy to see me, jumping up and down, dancing around, trying to get close enough to touch my red socks. Quite a few succeeded, as did a number of mothers and babies. It might appear to be almost a dangerous scene from outside, but from the centre where I was the crowd was so good-natured and happy that I never felt that the least harm could come to me.

I also liked the two temples I was taken to in Itumbaha. At the first temple, a very old, tumbling down courtyard (which is presently being completely restored), there were some ancient manuscripts in silver and gold, but unfortunately, that was all the explanation I was given, though I would have liked more. But of course, since I was expected to know everything, I was not allowed to just ask. It got crowded in the small courtyard of the temple as worshippers crowded in behind me, and the brother carrying me and I got jostled around quite a bit as we went back out through the narrow gateway into the larger courtyard. It was great fun. The second temple was the three Taras, white, green and red. They were pretty images, but I felt no kinship with them, since I knew I was alive and they were only images. Still, it was nice to know that they were there waiting for me every year.

The Itumbaha crowd was even bigger as we worked our way through it to the narrow gateway and back to the palanquin. The best part was over, but we were only just beginning, and there was still a long way to go as we continued along Kilagal then turned north toward Bangemudha and Tahity. These were two very crowded and exciting roads as we went past the toothache shrine and all the dentist shops with their grisly paintings of teeth, followed by shops selling prayer flags and other Buddhist items, mostly to Tibetans. But when we passed the small stupa in Tahity, we entered a completely different part of town: Thamel, the area that most tourists know best. Up to now, the shops had all been selling necessities: rice and sugar, *chiura* (beaten rice) and *achar* (pickles), pots and pans, medicine, and bales of cloth. But here everything changed and the shops began selling clothing, jewellery and more expensive religious statues and paintings, everything intended not for us, but for foreign visitors. There were many large, clean and bright eating places with signs written in the characters my teacher made me copy, but which I could make no sense of at all. What was most fun was the amazed look on the faces of the foreigners in the shops as they saw me carried unexpectedly by, a small girl in red and gold brocade looking extremely grave as she tried to keep from getting thrown out of her palanquin.

A turn east at the most crowded corner of Thamel, then north to Bhagwan Baha. Here a large crowd awaits me, but the courtyard is small, no more than a temple, so that we are squeezed to get in, pushed and shoved by the festive crowd. A band sits on the ground playing and there is hardly room to move around the courtyard, let alone the very narrow passages that lead in and out.

After the enthusiasm and size of the crowd at Bhagwan Baha, it is both a surprise and a relief to find the street nearly deserted as we head south through Jyatha towards Ason. The other two temples I visited in my early years came during this part of the journey, but I have no real memories of them. My carriers have been keeping up a brisk pace, and in spite of wishing that they could give me a smoother ride, I begin to feel sorry for them. But they seem enthusiastic enough as we re-enter one of the most crowded parts of town at Ason Tol, a square full of small temples where five roads meet. Here, people sit on the ground selling vegetables and leaves for making plates, while small shops sell rice, dal, dried fish of the kind used in the *sagun* ceremony, salt and tofu. In even smaller shops, spice vendors sell the many kinds of spices that make Nepali food so tasty.

From here, we take the road towards Indrachowk and Jan Baha, our last stop. This is one of the most interesting roads in the city, with shops crammed with everything from spices to religious images to baskets to clothing to garden tools and brass pots of every shape and size. The buildings look very old. One temple looks ready to collapse into the street, while another building has little terracotta soldiers marching all along it. Few people pay me much attention here in the commercial heart of the old city, and Jan Baha, where I am taken in to see Seto Machendranath is oddly deserted. Here there is no jostling, and I am carried straight up to see the image that I have last seen getting his annual bath at a much more raucous event.

It has been an exciting couple of hours, and now I am getting tired, glad that my temple is not much further away: through Indra Chowk with its ornate Akash Bhairav temple down Makhan Tol, past the Taleju Temple and Hanuman Dhoka. One of the best days of my year has come to an end. But in about three weeks, it will get even better.

Indra Jatra, which goes on for 9 days, is probably the biggest festival in the valley. Dasain is a more important family affair, but Indra Jatra is a great public spectacle, and so important was it for me, that it is sometimes called Kumari Jatra. It is supposed to mark the end of the monsoon, but since we go by the lunar calendar, it often rains quite heavily during the festival. This, as you will see, does not really dampen anyone's spirits.

Indra Jatra is a festival unique to the Kathmandu Valley, and commemorates an occasion when Indra had come down from heaven to pick flowers for his mother who wanted them for a puja. Being a god, he thought he could get away without asking permission, but was captured by the people of the valley, who regarded him as a thief. Even when they discovered who he was, the people would not let him go until his mother promised to pay them in silver. This "silver" took the form of the morning mists which come at the end of the monsoon and the beginning of autumn, and which are supposed to help the rice to ripen. This is the reason for the images of Indra that are taken out, and either tied up or put in little cages. These are seen all over the central part of town, and some of the images are so old, decayed and worm-eaten as to be scarcely recognizable. It is also the reason that a dancing elephant, actually two men behind a huge elephant mask, roams the streets. This is supposedly Indra's elephant looking for him. This is also the time when all the city's Bhairav heads are displayed, but no one ever told me why.[1]

---

[1] I later learned that Indra Jatra is combined with another festival commemorating the legend that an ancient Nepali king was slain by the Lord Krishna during a great battle in the Mahabharata. His head flew back to the Kathmandu Valley, and is thought to be the Akash Bhairav, a large blue Bhairav head with bulging eyes and long fangs, of Indra Chowk. As a goddess myself, I seem to have been expected to know about this without being told.

During this festival there are three occasions when I am pulled around on a huge chariot, which is actually a movable temple with a small three-story pagoda over where I sit. But I am not the only star. Two young boys, like me from the Shakya community, are chosen to be worshipped as Ganesh and Bhairav, and they proceed me in smaller chariots dressed almost as splendidly as I am. Ganesh is always the deity we worship first, and Bhairav, as a protector, goes in front of my chariot to clear the way. Dressed up, they look more similar to Kumari than they do to the gods they embody, and I have even seen photographs of one or another of them captioned "The Living Goddess" in articles in foreign magazines. Like me, they remain in their roles for a number of years, but their only public functions are during Indra Jatra and Dasain, unless anyone requests a special puja to worship the three of us. Unlike me, they live normal lives outside of festival times, attending school and staying with their families, the only concession to their divinity being that at meals they are always served first. But it is quite obvious who they are since they dress like Kumaris complete with eye makeup and top-knots, and are often mistaken for girls by people seeing them for the first time. The only difference is that instead of being dressed all in red, they wear a white tunic with a red sash. The criteria for selecting them are also less strict than for Kumari, and in fact they go in a hereditary family line. I never had any actual contact with the boys who were Ganesh and Bhairav during my time as Kumari, and am not even sure who they are in real life.

One thing I particularly liked about the festival was the way Taba's whole family, including all his brothers and their family, would gather at the Kumari Che. Then, of course, I thought of them as my real family, and it was wonderful having them around. Another feature of Indra Jatra was that I was not allowed to eat rice for the duration of the festival. My sisters asked me if I didn't mind this, but since Taba's family made me lots of tasty dishes without rice, like noodles and—one of my particular favourites—momos (streamed dumplings filled with chopped meat, vegetables and spices), it was no sacrifice for me at all.

The regular kitchen is not used during Indra Jatra. It is moved to the back part of the house. My kitchen with the platform where I ate my main meals, was locked for 8 days. However, even though I was not eating rice, I did not eat with the family during this time. The house was crowded, not only with relatives, but all sorts of people. Since it was not proper for me to eat with so many other people, I would eat either in the *Agan Kota* or in my bed room.

Just how Kumari became part of Indra Jatra is not precisely known, but it may be connected with yet another Kumari origin legend. In this one, a young girl, claiming to be a goddess, refused to behave with proper respect towards the king. Angered by this, the king banished her and her entire family, but the queen immediately became ill. Realising his mistake, the king brought her back and had her installed as the human emanation of Taleju. Some feel that the festival commemorates the triumphant return of the girl.

The festival actually began for me on the morning of the day before the 1st day. As well as the rest of the family I had to bathe, then all of our clothes and utensils were washed. In the late morning two elderly women from the palace arrived along with one or more of the Pancha Buddha, for *Nimantrana* (Invitation) Puja, a puja also offered to Ganesh and Bhairav. The two women offered me a new dress which I was to wear on the next day. It was after this puja that I could not eat rice for the duration of the festival.

On the evening before the festival began, in the long room next to the Singhasan, three long tables of offerings were laid out, consisting of no less than fifteen different kinds of roti and other snacks. One table was for Ganesh, one for Bhairav and one for me. Mine had to be three times as big as theirs. When we had looked them over and sampled them, the priest from the Taleju Temple made puja to my naga, one of only two times in the year when this is done (the other is after the final Indra Jatra chariot procession), and then we were taken over to the Taleju Temple, Ganesh and Bhairav carried by members of their own families. The square outside the Taleju Temple had a different feeling to it during Indra Jatra, because in the morning the massive Indra pole had been raised. This would stay up for the entire time of the festival. I never saw it raised or lowered during my time as Kumari since it was out of sight of my windows, but was told that it could be really frightening, swinging around on its ropes and threatening to fall on the crowd.

This short evening excursion was always more interesting than the other times I went no further than this because there was so much to look forward to in the next few days, but one year it was particularly special. I was still quite young, and barely remember it. What I do remember is that while I was being dressed, I complained that my father—who had always been a frequent visitor to Kumari Che, since his sister lived there—sometimes used to carry the previous Kumari at festivals, but since I had become Kumari, he had never carried me. When he heard about this, he decided he would be the one to carry me down the stairs and across the courtyard to the front door. From there I would walk the last few steps to the palanquin. However, when we got to the courtyard, no one could find the white cloth that I would have to walk on, and my father stood there holding me for nearly half an hour while everyone searched. There were some people with cameras in the courtyard, and the pictures of him holding me are some of my favourites. We look very happy together, even though I am not smiling in the photos. Eventually the cloth was found, right where it should have been all along, as if somehow it had been meant for us to spend this time together.

On the next day, the day of the first big procession (called *Kwoni ya* in Newari), Fufu or one of my sisters would start getting me ready about one o'clock, though the procession would not begin until three or four. On this day I would wear the dress that had been presented to me on the previous day by the two women from the palace. My head-dress was also much more elaborate, with real jewels, and very heavy. My necklaces, including, of course, the nine-coloured naga necklace, would be almost hidden by a garland of fragrant white ginger flowers. By the time I was fully made up even my own mother said she did not recognise me as her daughter, but could only think of me as a goddess. My sisters, who always came to Kumari Che before the processions said the same thing. The expression on my face in some of my pictures shows how I must have been feeling.

On this day, the whole royal family would watch the three of us—Ganesh, Bhairav and me—go off from the Ghadi Bhaitak, and the crowds would begin to gather and sit all over the temple steps from late morning. Because of the presence of the royal family, the square was kept in good order on the first day with plenty of police and guards keeping much of the area clear. Sometimes in the distance we could hear the "clang, clang, clang" of Lakhe's cymbal. Lakhe is one of the main dancers of the festival, a red demon (but a benevolent one), and the man dancing behind the mask is said to be in a trance. Even better was Indra's elephant who made a point of being completely out of control and dancing into the crowd. Though I knew I should soon see plenty of the dancers, who would be dancing in front of my chariot especially for me, my curiosity got the better of me, and whenever I could I would run over to a small window overlooking the square to see what was going on. The excitement of the square was just too much to resist.

Finally, when everything was ready, first Ganesh, then Bhairav would walk out of a side entrance of the Kumari Che and emerge from a neighbouring courtyard to walk with members of their families as attendants to their chariots which are parked behind mine. This is one time of year when I was really excited as

I waited my turn while a white cloth was laid out for me so that my feet would not touch the ground on the walk to my own chariot. Once I started walking, I was surrounded by thousands of equally excited people. What little girl wouldn't love dressing up and being the centre of so much attention? But of course I was not just a little girl, I was a goddess, the emanation of Taleju Bhawani, and I had to remain on my dignity through the photographers, and the people throwing flowers and coins and bowing down to me.

When I had walked to the chariot, I was lifted and handed up to my seat. As always, Gautam Dai and Mahendra Dai would be with me, not trying to keep me from falling off this time, but with a fan, for it was often hot and humid, and the cockpit of the chariot was cramped. Sometimes one or the other would support, or even lift my head-dress up to ease the burden on my neck.

When I was finally seated, a goat was sacrificed in front of the chariot, but this was out of sight from where I sat, and anyway was not sacrificed to me, but as a way of protecting the chariot for the journey. While I waited to be pulled off, Lakhe or the elephant would come and dance for me. I have often been asked how I managed not to laugh, especially at the elephant, and the fact is that I was laughing inside, but (though no one had ever told me) I knew I could not let it show.

Ganesh and Bhairav were now pulled out in front of me with a mighty cheer from the young pullers, who, like my own, were out to have a good time. Off they went across the square, proceeded by a fife and drum band, again dressed in black 18th century uniforms with turbans and white cross-belts. When my chariot was pulled forward, two soldiers, again dressed 18th century uniforms, fired off their muskets in salute. Then I made a brief stop before the King who made "Namaste" and threw me a coin (not a gold coin as the guidebooks sometimes say). Then I followed in the path of the smaller chariots on a round-about southern way via Lagan towards the neighbourhood where, by coincidence, my family lived. My sisters, who had been invited to the Kumari Che for the preparations, were by now running home so they could watch me go by. But they had plenty of time, for it would take me an hour or more to get there.

The chariot ride was like no other experience of the year. Unlike Bahi Dyah, when I saw people in the street going about their daily business, this was a totally festive atmosphere, and while the whole southern route of the first day could be walked in well under an hour, it would take many hours, and it would be quite dark, before we got back. Electricity was turned off all along the route, partly as a safety precaution, for the chariots were constantly running into electric or telephone poles and buildings on the narrow, pot-holed streets, and partially for atmosphere, for once it got dark the mood was special with the way lit by nothing more than votive lanterns.

Ganesh and Bhairav's chariots, being lighter, are easier to control, and got around the route much faster, though people worshipped them along the way as well. The young guys pulling mine seemed to want to get into just about every kind of mischief, sometimes jumping up and down on the shaft, at other times purposely running the chariot into a house or telephone pole. It was all part of the fun, and where the chariot got stuck people seemed to consider themselves fortunate to get such a good long look at Kumari. As for me, I was so fascinated by the whole scene that I did not care if it ever ended. In fact I was so caught up in the excitement that I usually didn't even notice that on the first day I was pulled right through the neighbourhood where my family lived. Of course I did not remember ever having lived there myself, but my sisters were always there watching me go by. Eventually when we did get back, there was another musket salute to celebrate my safe return, and as soon as I was inside, I would be offered *sagun* by one of the Pancha Buddha. They are always present at Indra Jatra, but my only contact with them is at *Nimantrana* Puja, and being offered *sagun* by one of them at the end of each procession.

This was still only the beginning, for there were two more processions (*Thani ya* and *Nanicha ya*), this time through the northern end of town. On these occasions I would wear my best dress with real silver and gold brocade thread. This dress was presented to me by the government when I was installed as Kumari, and would be the only item of dress or jewellery that I would be allowed to keep when I retired. There was no one from the royal family on these days, so the square was a lot more exciting and disorganised, but like before, Ganesh and Bhairav went in front of me and two muskets were fired off when I was pulled away. The second procession was by far the longest, heading north then turning east to Bangemudha and Ason. There were frequent stops for Lakhe and the elephant to dance for me, and by now the elephant's mask was beginning to look a little dented from all the things he had run into. I am told that when I was very young that this procession was so long that sometimes I fell asleep, especially if we were stuck for a long time. It is hard to believe because in my later years I used to enjoy every minute. On the way back, we stopped in front of Seto Bhairav, a huge golden Bhairav face in the walls of Hanuman Dhoka, which is only open during this festival. *Chang*, a local rice beer, flows from a reed in his mouth and young guys fight to get some of it because it is said to bring them good luck in the coming year. They seemed to fight especially hard when I was watching.

There is an event one year in particular that I remember during this, the longest procession. I think I was about 8 or 9. Suddenly there was a very heavy rain. So heavy in fact that the pullers ran for cover, and all my young cousins on the chariot abandoned it and started jumping through windows. The chariot is quite high off the ground, and at about the level of first floor windows. Normally, of course, people don't allow strangers to climb in their windows, but in this case, everyone was such a good mood that out of respect for Kumari, they not only let all these young men in, but offered them soft drinks and snacks. These offerings were held up for me (along with Gautam and Mahendra who had not abandoned me) to see. When we eventually got back to Kumari Che they all thanked me. "Dyah Meiju, because of the rain and because of you, we got to flirt with the pretty girls who had come to see you."

There is a gap of up to five days, depending on the year's calendar, between the second and third processions during which life returns more or less to normal for me. I can't eat rice, but I can still look out the windows at the waiting chariots and the occasional dancers. Whenever the chariots were not actually in use, I could see other kids playing on them like they were playground equipment.

The third procession is shorter, going only as far north as Kilagal, past Itumbaha then back through Indra Chowk. This procession was supposedly added at a later date for the benefit of a Malla king's concubine who lived along the route. I didn't know this at the time, and certainly wouldn't have known what a concubine was. But the real significance of this day was that after I got back, the king used to come for his annual tika from me. This is an important ceremony for the king and in fact for the nation. It not only bestows good fortune on the kingdom for the coming year, but some say I am giving permission for a non-Newar king to rule over us for another year. This is of course what happened at that famous Indra Jatra of 1768 when Prithvi Narayan Shah got the tika instead of Jayaprakash Malla. And everyone has heard the story of how when King Tribhuvan came for his Tika in 1954, the Kumari seemed disoriented and confused and somehow gave it to his son Mahendra instead. Within a year the crown prince was king, his father having died in Switzerland, where he had gone for medical treatment.

Normally, after the procession, I went to the golden naga throne and waited for the king there. When he arrived he would give me a gold one rupee coin (which went into the Kumari treasury), and I in turn gave him a tika three times with my left hand. For young girls, the left hand is considered the purest, and it was only the king who got a tika from my left hand, perhaps because I used my right hand for commoners. We never spoke, but before he left, the king would ask Taba if there were any problems or special needs. The queen, by the way, is never allowed in the Kumari Che. This is because of the story that it was the jealousy of the queen that led to Taleju's refusal to appear before the king and to the establishment of the Kumari cult.

One year, I can't remember exactly when, though I was still quite young, King Birendra varied the routine by purposely arriving early. Perhaps he just wanted to feel what it would be like to stand on the street like a normal person, but at any rate, he arrived about ten or fifteen minutes before I did and just stood there waiting for me. I'll always remember the way he stood there looking at me as the chariot pulled up.

Indra Jatra was my biggest festival of the year, and I was always sorry when it was over. Not long after, there was a mysterious little event at which I had to be present when the image of a deity called Pachali Bhairav was brought to Hanuman Dhoka. As with Changu Narayan, he was brought in the form of a pot, a golden one this time, and it was always late at night. As with most of my smaller festivals, no one ever knew exactly when this one was going to take place, but while I was allowed to go to sleep, the rest of the family had to stay up, or we might miss the whole thing. This was the only occasion when I was dressed up first, since I had to be ready as soon as I was woken up. Sometimes it could be quite cold at that time of night as well, so that I was reluctant to get out of my warm bed. Though it always excited me to see a sacred image, even if it was only represented by a pot, this is the one time of year when I would have happily slept through an excursion outside.

While Indra Jatra is a great public spectacle, for most Nepalis the most important festival of the year is Dasain. This is the time when families get together if at all possible, and if people can only afford to eat meat once during the year, this will be the time they save up to do it.

I was only involved in Dasain on one night, Kal Ratri, or the 9th night. That is a very special night, for not only are Ganesh and Bhairav present for the only time except Indra Jatra, but there are nine little temporary Kumaris chosen and brought to the Kumari Che, so that there are ten Kumaris present. These Ga[1] Kumari (*ga* means "group" in Newari) are also from the Shakya caste, and in order to be eligible must not yet have done their *ihi*, or bel fruit marriage, ceremony. It is said that if you are made Ga Kumari, you will be healthy for an entire year, and in fact some girls are put forward because they have been ill, as being made Ga Kumari for a day is thought of as a way to cure them. All my sisters were Ga Kumaris while I was Royal Kumari: Pramila once, Surmila—who always seems to get the most of everything—5 or 6 times, Samjhana 3 times and Sunila twice.

It was always nice to know that one or more of my sisters was there. Having them made up as little Kumaris seemed to make something clearer in our ambivalent relationship. But I was not allowed to see them. They were always kept on the upper floor, while I was on the one below, though worshippers would come to worship all of us. The reason I could not see them was that on that day I wore my golden third eye and was considered at my most powerful.[2] The Gan Kumaris wore silver third eyes, and it

---

[1] Like *che*, *ga* is pronounced with a nasilised sound at the end and would probably be more correctly spelled ga(n).

[2] Guidebooks and articles invariably say that the third eye is "painted" on and that Kumari wears it every day. If you look closely at the photographs, you will notice that the third eye Kumari wears for festivals is made of gold with only the pupil painted in. On normal days she wears only a tika.

is thought that if we looked eye to eye it would cause serious problems for the Gan Kumaris.

As part of the ceremony, we were worshipped by a Dyah-Ma, an elderly woman who would become possessed by a goddess and go into a trance. My sisters later described how frightening this was for them, as the woman trembled and touched their feet with her cold, shivering hands. But though I went through the same experience, I didn't find it at all frightening. People were always worshipping me, and if one of the worshippers was a little different, so what? It is not as if anyone could, or would, harm the earthly incarnation of Taleju.

Now came the mysterious ceremony that has led to one of the biggest misunderstandings about Kumari, when I was taken into the room with all the severed buffalo heads late at night. But first I had to get from my temple to the Taleju Mandir, and this was the part of the entire evening that I enjoyed most. It was always about 11 PM or midnight, and though the same thing happened every year, few people were interested enough to come out and watch, so that the streets were deserted. At other festivals I was carried, and this was the only time of the year that I got to walk any distance. It was on a white cloth, of course, since my feet could never touch the ground, but it was thoroughly enjoyable. The weather in October is not too cold, and it never rains then, so it was perfect for my stroll, and because it was so silent, all along the way I could hear the jingling of my silver *ghanjla*, or anklets. It may not sound like much, but imagine how thrilling this would be to a child who never gets to walk anywhere outside. It was much more important to me personally than what came next.

When I arrived at the Taleju Temple the priest (Achaju: the dignified old man, not the one whose bag we hid) washed my feet, and the water from that was sprinkled all over the people who were there. Then I entered the Taleju Temple and had to pass through the room where the heads of some recently sacrificed buffalo were kept. As far as I remember, there were only eight or ten heads, certainly not 108. The room was dark, lit only by a single tiny oil lamp, not to be frightening, but because no one else is allowed to view the scene. The puja is one of our most secret ceremonies, though it only lasts for about five to ten minutes. I was never afraid then, it was simply one of my many duties, though I do not know if I could do it now.

It is important to remember that this has nothing to do with the selection of a Kumari, as almost every book or article mistakenly claims. This is a ceremony that all Kumaris have to go through every year, although since Dasain is considered the ideal time to change Kumaris, this is sometimes a new Kumari's first duty. There is never any deliberate attempt to frighten a Kumari, and I have never heard of one being afraid or crying, but I have also never heard that this would cause her to lose her divinity if it did happen.

Although this was my only public duty during Dasain, the next day came one that was important to my family, especially to my father and mother. On the final day of Dasain, all over Nepal children receive tika from their parents. But with us, because of my divine status, the usual order of things was reversed, and just as I gave a tika to the king once a year, so on this day, I would give it to my family.

Of all the other gods and goddesses in Kathmandu, the one I come into contact with most frequently was Seto Machendranath, a rather charming little white image believed by Buddhists to be an emanation of Lokeshwar, the Bodhisattva of Compassion, and by Hindus to represent the Lord Goraknath, whose main shrine is in the Kashthamandap, the huge wooden building in Durbar Square said to have been built from a single tree. I came face to face with him three times during the course of the year. One of those occasions was Bahi Dyah, which I described earlier. Another was on the occasion of his annual bath. This was an enjoyable time for several reasons. One was the atmosphere in the temple courtyard. I was brought to Jan Baha, and I sat off to the side, while the image of Seto Machendranath was brought out of the temple and placed a little way off from me in the courtyard. Though the bath could not take place until I had arrived, and people did come to worship me as well, I was not the main attraction. I was more like a master of ceremonies, and was surrounded by people and children running around and playing. One year it was the closest I came to my two foreign friends, as they were allowed to come and stand by me, though they were lectured beforehand by Gautam and Mahendra on how they were not to make me laugh.

Seto Machendranath wears 108 separate items of clothing, and it was fun watching the splendid robes all being taken off him, until he stood looking rather forlorn, though he did keep his crown. Then three of his priests each dumped a jug of milk over him as trumpets blared and the crowd cheered. This was followed first by jugs of hot water from the Vishnumati River, which flows to the west of the old city, and finally with cold water from the same river. The ceremony happens in mid-winter, and in fact it may be a little colder on the day of his bath since we believe that it always rains for three or four days at the time of the festival, and I felt a little sorry for him, though I knew he was only an image. After his bath, I was taken home, though he would remain in the courtyard for a further week while he was repainted. I was sorry that I couldn't see that, for while only a trained religious artist is skilful enough to paint him, no one but his priests of the Bajracharya caste are holy enough to touch him, so that the painter sits next to the priest and tells him exactly what to do.

During January or February I would again be taken out to meet Changu Narayan at the gate of the Taleju Temple. This brief ceremony was exactly like the one during the monsoon except now the weather was much cooler and all my finery was more comfortable.

The next time I was taken out was for a ceremony that was almost exactly the same except that in the intervening month or so it had become much warmer. It was called Chaitya Dasain, and it was so similar to the two Changu Narayan pujas that I always confuse the three of them.

A festival that always disappointed me was Ghoda Jatra, the Horse Festival. It had a lot of possibilities, but never lived up to them. The best thing about it was the horse. I didn't get to ride it, of course, but it followed along behind my palanquin. This is Taleju's horse, and if you peek into the courtyard of Hanuman Dhoka in the mornings when visitors are not allowed except to do puja, you will see her wandering around freely.

Our destination was the Tundikel, or parade ground at the far end of New Road, the largest open space in Kathmandu, where there would be a big military parade with horse races, and parachute jumps. The problem was that instead of being on the field where the action took place, I was stuck in the RNAC (Royal Nepal Airlines Corporation) Building across the road. Not only was the road wide enough to put me a good way off, but there was a big tree in the way, so that to see anything I had to look through the leaves. So while the day should have been a treat for me, I always wound up feeling a bit cheated. I've noticed that the tree is no longer there, so perhaps later Kumaris have had a better time.

The next time that I was supposed to come face to face with Seto Machendranath was during his chariot festival, which is also called Laganya in Newari because the destination of the chariot is Lagan Tole where the 200-year-old palace of a once all-powerful Prime Minister named Bhim Sen Thapa stands. What I particularly liked about this festival was that although I was present, I had no official function, no one bothered to worship me on that day, so that I felt like one of the crowd, and this was really the only time of the year that I was able to feel that way. I used to watch from the windows of the Kumari Che as Seto

Machendranath's chariot was pulled by, then I was taken to Lagan Tole on my palanquin by another route, via Basantapur, Jhoche and Yangal. The only trouble was that the young men pulling Seto Machendranath's chariot were as mischievous as the ones who pulled my own during Indra Jatra, and the result was that it usually got stuck somewhere. So stuck that it would often not arrive at Lagan before I had to go back to my own temple. Of the eight years I was Kumari, I can only remember three when the chariot actually showed up and I could enjoy the spectacle just like anyone else. The other years I was disappointed.

During my years as Kumari, there was one special event called Baha Puja, though I must have been very young at the time since I do not remember it very well. It is an event which is not held regularly, when worshippers go around to all the *baha* and *bahi* (Buddhist courtyards) of Kathmandu. As the deity of Kumari Che, I was brought into the courtyard and seated on the left so that worshippers could file through and do puja to me.

And so the years went by. Most of my days were normal enough: *Nitya* Puja every morning, the more complex *Dasami* Puja performed by one of the Pancha Buddha on the 10th day of some months, a worshipper or two every day in normal times with far more during Dasain and Indra Jatra, an abbreviated lesson, solitary meals, playmates who had to play whatever I wanted them to, and of course, my dolls. The festivals were really special times, and the older I became, the more I enjoyed them. But even a goddess grows up, and as the time passed there were some small changes in my life.

4

Each child generally serves three or four years, and then falls back into the mass again.

– H. Ambrose Oldfield,
Sketches from Nepal, 1880

Early in the year 1990, something strange began happening to me. During the entire time I had been Kumari, I had not once been ill, but I now began to have a strange fever. It was not a high one, and there was no question of calling a doctor, but it did make me moody, and I amazed everyone in the Kumari Che by sudden and unexplained fits of weeping. I had always been a happy child, even in my pre-Kumari days, and had not cried once that anyone could remember since my installation.

At the same time, interesting things were happening in the streets, and when I felt well enough—and was not having a crying fit—I was at the windows looking out into the square, or even out into the narrow alleyway in the back. For at this time the streets were full of people, fighting with the police and demonstrating for something called "democracy". I didn't know what it was, but could not help but hear the word bandied about. Whatever it was, I don't think Taba and Fufu much approved of it, for Kumari had a very special relationship with the king.

For a while there was a curfew, and people were only allowed on the streets for one hour a day to do their shopping. This made my days boring, though *Nitya* Puja was still done and a few worshippers who lived nearby hurried in to do puja. But for the rest of the day there was nothing to see but police patrols, although the hurry, hustle and bustle of the one hour of activity almost made up for it. In my childish innocence, I thought the people rushing around to buy whatever they could in an hour were hilarious.

More serious was the time the fighting overflowed from New Road into Basantapur and Durbar Square. From the windows I could see the crowd throwing bricks and stones at the police. There were explosions, a strange smell, and a crowd went running towards the alleyway. I rushed to the back to try and see what was going on and was surprised to see people throwing buckets of water on the fleeing demonstrators. Excited, I ran to the lounge where I hoped to find some of the family, and blurted out what I had seen. "It's to help with the tear gas," explained Mahendra, "The water makes the people feel better." For no reason at all, I broke out into tears.

A day or two later everyone was clustered around the TV. "The king has given up power," Taba explained to me. "The people will vote for their government. The king will live in the palace, but he will no longer rule." He looked at me intently. "You must have felt something, Dyah Meiju. That was the reason for the tears and the fever. It is just like the time Kumari gave the tika to Crown Prince Mahendra instead of to King Tribhuvan." Whether that was true or not, the fevers and the crying spells stopped. Some accounts will tell you that weeping disqualifies a Kumari, but as far as I know, there was no talk of replacing me at this time.

Over the years my lessons did not improve. At the age of twelve I was a whiz at multiplication tables, and my spoken Nepali was as good as my Newari, but I could hardly read. In English, I could only recognise the capital letters and, in common with my teacher, could not say or understand a word. Pramila sometimes tried to help me on the rare occasions when she could get my attention, in particular explaining a long involved story in my Nepali book about a father, a son and a donkey, that would later become a kind of family legend.

My behaviour towards my younger sisters was now a little better. In an effort to get closer to me, my sisters sometimes spent the night at Kumari Che, but though I still preferred the company of Taba's grandchildren and my other cousins, I found that I was beginning to miss my sisters when they went away. Sometimes I even called to them from the windows not to go away and leave me. I still tended to keep Pramila at a distance, however, perhaps because she was older and a bit of an authority figure. I hardly ever spoke to Surmila, though she once asked me why I was so stuck-up, and warned me that I would have to behave like a proper sister once I went home. And I would not know for a long time that the way I behaved toward my mother before my brother was born had sometimes caused her to go home and cry.

Whatever my failings as daughter and sister, I never once doubted my power. The boy who could not speak was cured after about three weeks of pujas, and the blood-vomiting journalist recovered after his forgiveness puja.[1] Judging from the number of offerings I got from other grateful mothers, I must have assisted with any number of problems that I never even really knew about, since normally the mothers did not bring their children and of course they never spoke to me directly about what they wanted. Both my brothers in Kumari Che had consulted me over their marriages, showing me photographs of their prospective brides and asking if I approved. I think that if I hadn't liked the looks of the girls, they would have looked for someone else. An important politician had even come seeking help, but neither had I heard of him, nor did I understand anything of his problem. Yet that did not mean that I wasn't sure I could help him. I had a self-confidence almost unheard of in a child my age and never had any

---

[1] I should confess to telescoping these two incidents in Chapter 2. In reality they were a couple of years apart.

worries or fears the entire time I lived in Kumari Che. They would come later.

Even as indulged as I was, I gradually became a little more independent within the confines of my life. It is not necessarily true that a Kumari is waited on to the point where she is incapable of doing anything for herself. I dressed myself, except for festivals, and if everyone was too busy, I sometimes combed and tied up my own hair. I also graduated from the messes I cooked for my dolls to making tea and snacks for myself—fried potatoes and instant vegetable noodles were my favourites—so that I was not completely useless in the kitchen, though there was always someone to clean up after me.

Then came the day when Pramila came to tell me that a new Kumari had been selected and that I would soon be coming home. On that day I just went back to playing on the swing and really did not think about it very much. Perhaps because I was incapable of imagining another life, the thought of losing the one I had did not greatly trouble me. During that week a little girl named Ameeta Shakya came to visit once or twice. I took no notice of her, though I knew that she would take over from me. It was not that I was jealous or resentful. After all, I had taken over from the previous Kumari. That was what the world was like. She was just too young and small to be worth noticing. But I did listen in on Taba's conversations with her. I don't remember what he said, only that he was already beginning to treat her in the same kind and gentle way he always treated me.

My sisters seemed excited during my final week when they came to visit me, and didn't even notice whether I paid them any mind or not. "Father is having the whole inside of the house painted, just so you won't be disappointed by how old it is," Pramila told me.

"And guess what?" interrupted Surmila. "We're buying a TV! Oh, it's just a tiny black and white one, nothing like you have here. Father says it's all we can afford, but it's better than nothing. I'm so glad you're coming home!"

"Oh, shush, that's not important," admonished Pramila, then turned to me. "Father is very happy. I think he has always missed not having you at home."

"But mother is worried that you are going to be just as ...." a stern look from her older sister caused Surmila to bite back her words. After all, I was still Dyah Meiju, and what she was saying bordered on a rebuke.

What I did not know was that I had been the subject of some intense family discussions for some time. My family is the sort that gets together and talks out its problems, and my behaviour towards them was thought to be a problem worthy of discussion. My mother and father were particularly worried about how I would behave when I came back because they had seen former Kumaris and the difficulties they had had in adjusting.

While my family is not poor, it is not rich either, and with 6 children there were bound to be difficulties and conflicts. They realised that I had never had to struggle or compromise, that I was accustomed to just giving orders, and that I would not be able to survive if I kept thinking like this. And so they made the conscious decision to make an effort to turn me into a normal girl. They knew it could not be done all at once, and they knew that I couldn't be forced. My parents had plenty of experience bringing up children, and they thought that my two older sisters would be my best guides. But of course this was all in the future.

I was only officially informed by Taba one day before I was to leave. It was now the middle of the Dasain Festival, and I learned that this year I would not be walking late at night to the Taleju Temple, so would not be able to hear my bangles jingling. The new Dyah Meiju would do that as her first official duty. This is often the case, Dasain being the ideal time to change Kumaris (though I had taken office during the Holi festival in the spring), and has contributed to the myth of this being part of the selection process.

The next day, the 8th day of Dasain, as soon as *Nitya* Puja was finished, I began to be dressed in all my most special finery, the things I normally wore only for Indra Jatra: the gold and silver brocaded dress, all of my golden jewellery except for the naga necklace, and even the special jewelled crown. My family arrived about 11 am, Father looking proud and pleased, Pramila stern and important, Surmila like she was about to crack a joke, and the younger ones—Samjhana, Sunila and Sarbagya all very excited and giggling. My mother waited at home to welcome me with a puja. Like me, they were all dressed in their best; my father in a suit, all the girls in spotless, pressed *salwar khameez*, and my little brother in a miniature suit. In contrast to the holiday mood of my real family, everyone in my caretaker family, from Taba right down to his grandchildren, was in tears. I felt like crying myself, though I knew that this was unthinkable in my position. But I was unable to speak to anyone either.

First there was the ceremony of handing over my Naga necklace to the new little Kumari. The ceremony itself is secret (as is the room where it takes place) with only four people present: the two girls, the caretaker and the Achaju, the priest from the Taleju Temple, who performed the actual handover. Oddly enough, I felt no strong emotion. Perhaps that was because even though this little ceremony symbolised the handing over of my divinity, for the next few days I was still to dress as Kumari and be regarded as such since I was thought to still retain some power during that time.

Now it was time to take me "home". It felt a little strange being in my full Indra Jatra regalia minus my naga necklace and the feeling of power that went with it. What even felt stranger was wearing all this but getting into my palanquin rather than my chariot. The route, however should have been familiar, for it was the beginning of the one my chariot was pulled on during the first Indra Jatra procession, around the Narayan Temple, in front of the Kashthamandap, then down a street lined with shops. Especially sweet shops, I noticed. It was in another way like one of my minor festivals, with no one expecting me to pass by, and surprise registering on most people's faces. I remember my crown being unusually heavy, for on the chariot one of my brothers would sometimes support the weight, but there was no way they could do this on the palanquin. Still, the novelty of the scene kept me from noticing it very much.

The journey was not long, ten or fifteen minutes. We reached a large temple where my chariot had always turned left, but where we turned right down a hill. Then the palanquin was set down, I was picked up by Mahendra and carried through a couple of nondescript courtyards to the door of a very old looking house. Not a separate house, of course, but just one built into all the others. At the door, my mother, who had been waiting, performed a *laskus*, or welcome puja. Since this was done whenever I returned to Kumari Che after an Indra Jatra procession, I was familiar with it, the only novelty being that it was performed by my mother, and it did not seem strange that it was done in a new place.

The ceremonies were not over yet. After I was carried up a steep, narrow wooden staircase, not unlike the ones I was used to, I was taken to a rectangular room and placed on a bed at one end. Then I was offered *Sagun*, to indicate that I had completed my journey. As soon as I had touched the boiled egg, dried fish and *raksi* to my lips, everyone wanted to have their photos taken with me, and I felt I was a little unceremoniously shuffled from one sister to another. I certainly look a little disoriented in the photos. Everyone was so anxious for the photos because now I had to give all my jewellery back. First the heavy crown came off, then the various necklaces, golden chain, pearls, bracelets and anklets. The only thing I was allowed to keep was the dress, for that had been presented to me eight years before by the government.

Looking back, I am surprised that giving back the jewellery was not more upsetting, but at the time it seemed no different from taking it off after a procession.

And then the people from Kumari Che left, and I suddenly found myself alone among strangers. Of course they were not complete strangers. They had been visiting me for the last eight years, but they did not seem like my family, the people I should be living with. I sat on my bed and said nothing. I had changed my dress into the plain red cotton that I always wore as Kumari, I still had my eye make-up on and my hair tied up in a red ribbon, but I was in the wrong place.

I looked around, trying to find some comfort. The house didn't look all *that* old. It had just been painted, and the room I was in was brighter than many of the rooms at Kumari Che. But it was small. All the rooms I had seen were small. There was no glass in the windows, but there was no glass in the windows of Kumari Che either. I looked out straight at another old building, and could see no more than the corner of a plain courtyard. Where was Durbar Square with its constant activity, or my beautiful courtyard where people from all over the world came to see me? Was this mean little hovel to be my home?

"Would Dyah Meiju like to eat?" It was my mother, breaking in on my unhappy thoughts. I did not react. Taking this for assent, she brought me a tray with some of my favourite dishes: fish cooked with tomato, a tasty duck-egg omelette made with *chiura*, and of course tomato *achar*. I was served alone, sitting on my bed, much as I had sat on my platform in Kumari Che. Just as well. Why would I want to eat with *them*? If I was still wearing red and they were calling me Dyah Meiju, then they could continue to treat me as a goddess.

I looked at the food with distaste. I knew that it had been prepared especially for me. These were the same dishes they had brought me every Dasain, and while I was usually indifferent to my family, I had always looked forward to the food, for I had to admit there were some things that my mother made better than anyone else. But today these special dishes might as well have been stale *roti* or burnt rice. I took a bite or two and turned away. Later when my mother came in and saw the food hardly touched, she looked hurt. But though she said nothing to me, she has a naturally loud voice, and from another room I could here her complaining, "And just what is wrong with my food today, I'd like to know? All her favourites and hardly touched."

I could hear them all eating in another room, but their voices were too indistinct to hear if they were talking about me. My grandmother came and sat with me. It was comforting to have her there because she did not attempt to talk with me.

"Would Dyah Meiju like to watch television?" asked Surmila hopefully. I sat looking out the window, trying to imagine Durbar Square until she went away.

"Would Dyah Meiju like to read something with me?" This was Pramila. Would they never give up?

Later, people from the neighbourhood came to do puja to me. This was at least something familiar, but it was also sad because it was in the wrong place. At any rate it kept people from trying to talk to me and gave me an excuse to sit for hours without moving, thinking of my home, my real home, and wishing I was there. I had been told that after four days, I would be able to go back and visit. If I just sat here for long enough the four days would pass.

But I was not allowed to sit for long. This was the 8th day of Dasain, *Maha Astami* (or *Kuchive* in Newari), and on that day there is a family ceremony when everyone is supposed to sit in order of their age. I should have sat between Surmila and Samjhana, but since I was still being treated as a goddess, they didn't know where to put me. Finally they just decided to sit me separately.

Dinner came eventually, but I still had no appetite. "Like this Dyah Meiju," said Surmila, sitting opposite me, taking a big handful of rice and stuffing it into her mouth. Everyone seemed to think that was funny, so she did it again.

"Humph! Not good enough for her, I wonder?" I could hear my mother in the distance, though she said nothing in my presence.

Before I went to bed of course I had to use the toilet that I would now share with everyone, and wash my face in a place also shared by everyone else. How disgusting! I had never had to share these things before. I had been interested in seeing the house, but now I had seen enough. I could hardly believe that I would have to sleep here. In fact I didn't sleep very much. I was so filled with unhappiness, and an uneasiness I did not recognise. I remember crying, but I think my father, who came to console me, was the only one who knew. My only consolation was that I was one day closer to my return visit.

There was a lot of activity around the house the next day. It was *Maha Nahomi*, the 9th day of Dasain, when traditionally families go around visiting and doing puja at various temples. I was still not supposed to go outside, so half the family went out at a time. It didn't matter to me, and I spent as much time as I could staring at the little black and white TV screen. I again ate very little, and in the afternoon Pramila came to plead with me. "Could not Dyah Meiju try to eat a little to please Mother? Everything she makes is so good, and she has been making a special effort for you. She is becoming worried." I shook my head to indicate that, yes, maybe I would try.

During the afternoon I cheered up a little when one of my playmates was sent from Kumari Che to bring some of my dolls. I was so happy to see her that I broke into a big smile. She stayed for a while and we played together with my dolls. That evening when everyone returned from their temple visits, I made more of an effort to eat, but still did not finish very much.

Before bed time I went down to the toilet as silently as I could, and as I passed the door to the room on the first floor, heard my sisters talking. Unable to resist, I stopped and eavesdropped.

"This has been a big disappointment so far!" It was Surmila, always forthright when she wasn't joking. "All she does is sit there, like she is too good for us."

"But we have to try and understand," answered Pramila, surprising me by coming to my defence. "Her life has been so different. It must be hard for her."

"The food is great. Even better than usual in Dasain," piped in Samjhana, who was now about 10.

"That's true enough," said Surmila, who loved a good meal. "But poor Mother is beside herself. She is not cooking these delicacies for us, you know, although we get the leftovers. I just hope she livens up. We were all excited, thinking we were getting a new sister. She won't even watch television with us."

I had heard enough, and fearful of getting caught, I descended silently to the ground floor. What business was it of theirs, anyway?

On my third day home, the 10th day of Dasain, I gave my family tika as I always had. That reminded me a little of my old life, but then they all went off in shifts to get another tika from the new Kumari. Sometime during the afternoon, my sorrow overwhelmed me, even though I knew that on the next day I would be able to go home. But would it be the same? I knew that I would not be able to keep myself from crying. I was not used to crying, and except for that strange brief period toward the end of the democracy movement, and the first night at home in bed, I could not remember ever having done it. I did not want anyone to see this, so I put a pillow over my face and was as silent as I could be. How long it went on I don't know, but I remember looking up to see Pramila staring at me. "Don't tell anyone," I begged her. She put her fingers to her lips to indicate that she would be silent, and went out of the room.

Crying had made me feel a little better, but more important was the knowledge that on the next day I would see my home again.

The next day was much busier. In the morning the familiar figure of Guruju, one of the five Pancha Buddha, arrived and performed puja with me for the last time. Then the family offered me *sagun*, for the final time as a goddess. After that my hair was taken down. It would never be pulled up tightly in a bun again, though I still like it tied back. My family now gave me a new dress, still red so that I would feel comfortable in it, and I went into another room to change. Following the change of hair style and clothes, I was offered *sagun* again. This time it was offered to *me*, not to Kumari, and strictly speaking, from this time on I was no longer a goddess.

Now came a real adventure, as I returned to the Kumari Che, not carried or pulled, but under my own steam. Gautam and Mahendra came around to get me ("Look at her smiling at them when we haven't had a smile in four days!" commented Surmila) along with some other cousins. I went downstairs and for the first time in eight years put on shoes. As Kumari I had not even been allowed to touch anyone wearing leather, so the shoes were synthetic. They felt strange. In fact they hurt, but I didn't mind because of the novelty.

Of course I was accustomed to walking around the inside of my temple, and now my house, but except for Kal Ratri, I never walked outside, and even then I had walked on a white cloth. Walking first across the courtyard, and then along a street, was a very different experience. I put one foot down carefully, then the other, making sure the front one was firmly planted before lifting the back one. It was a bit slow, but seemed to work, and no one corrected me. Climbing the hill to the temple was hard. I felt like I should be holding someone's hand, but was too embarrassed to ask. Gautam and Mahendra joked that they should carry me since I didn't know how to walk properly, and everyone laughed. We turned off onto a street that was crowded with people walking, rickshaws and the occasional tuk-tuk. Shops sold big red slabs of meat, newspapers and cold drinks. Men were having their hair cut in tiny shops, while women sat on the steps of temples selling vegetables.

Between learning to walk in shoes and being so fascinated by everything that was going on, I did not have time to notice just where we were or what route we were taking. We attracted a little attention because there were so many of us, but no one seemed to recognise the girl clomping carefully along the street picking out each step, and for the first time that I could remember when I had been outside, no one offered me flowers or coins, and no one wanted to touch my feet. We passed a row of sweet shops, and it occurred to me that if I wanted to, and if I had any money, I could just walk in and buy whatever I wanted. What a nice thought it was.

I have never been so happy to arrive anywhere as at my old home where I had lived for eight years. The four days at home had seemed like four decades. Now I could relax among people I knew. The kindness of my sisters and brother and my mother's consideration as she tried to make foods that I would enjoy had made no impression on me at all. This was where I wanted to be, and there were still a lot of people around since it was the end of Dasain.

In a way it is odd that I *did* feel so much at home when I went back. At my new home I had still been treated as Kumari for the past four days, but here I was now treated as one of the family. No one came to worship me. Most important, I did not eat main meals on the raised platform in my old kitchen by myself, but with the family. It was the first time I could remember that I had ever eaten proper meals as part of a group, and not off to the side. My appetite had returned almost as soon as I walked through the door, but at meal times I found it difficult to find time to get the food in my mouth, so busy was I talking and laughing with everyone. They still called me Dyah Meiju, but I knew it was only a courtesy. The real Dyah Meiju was the tiny girl in red eating on her raised platform by herself. I didn't mind not being goddess and centre of attention anymore as long as I was where I considered home. At night I slept in my old room, but on the floor, not on my old bed, and was quite content. I ignored the new Dyah Meiju. I wasn't jealous, but she just did not seem important, and she was asleep anyway by the time I went to bed.

But of course it had to end. A few evenings later my father came to get me after he had finished work.

"I don't want to go," I insisted. I was surprised that I had worked up the courage to say it. My father is someone who, like the Achaju, commands respect. He is also naturally cheerful, and easy going. He just smiled at me and did not get angry.

"But you must go, Dyah Meiju," said one of my brothers, to my surprise. "You are always welcome here, but this is not your home anymore. It is time to grow up."

"Can I come back sometimes?" I asked my father, not really trusting my voice not to break.

"Of course you can," answered my father gently. "Now let's go. Your sisters are waiting for you." I understood, though he did not say it, that I would no longer sit on my bed and eat by myself. From that night, I would be expected to be part of the family. I tried to put on a brave face, but Pramila later told me that I looked very angry when I came back. It was after 8, and I just went to bed without speaking to anyone.

In fact, over the next few weeks I saw very little of anyone except my mother. Dasain was now over. My sisters and brother all put on their school uniforms, slung their packs on their backs, went off to school every morning, and didn't come back until after 4. Father went to work. Mother did not seem to quite know what to do with me. Former Kumaris are sometimes not asked to do any housework by their families. Indeed, the more conservative among our community think it is positively wrong for an ex-goddess to do any sort of manual work. My mother would later prove to handle a difficult daughter very well, but at this point we were all a bit confused about just what my role in the family should be.

And I was bored stiff. It was October, mid-semester, and an awkward time to start school since admission only takes place in February, and no one knew what grade I should go into anyhow. I had nothing to do all day except play with my dolls and watch a bit of TV, or take out all the gifts I had received as Kumari. I was still too shy to go outside by myself. Sometimes I got so bored that I tidied the room, just to have something to do.

You would have thought that I would be so desperate for company that I would be glad to see my sisters when they came home from school and to hear their news, but I remained shy and withdrawn. Though I joined the family for meals, I sat off by myself and did not join in the conversations. It was not like when I had gone back to Kumari Che and had lots to talk about with people I knew well. This family talked about things I knew nothing of. In fact their constant chatter about their alien world sometimes got on my nerves, and there were occasions when I just asked them to shut up. In these early days they would still do what I asked them to avoid upsetting me.

One night I got so frustrated that I announced that I was going back to Kumari Che. Nobody paid any attention to me.

"I will, you know!" I insisted standing up.

"Go ahead. Who's stopping you?" asked Surmila.

I just stood there glaring at everyone.

"Are you still here?" Asked Surmila sarcastically. "I thought you were going."

"I ... I don't know the way!" I blurted out, and broke down in tears.

At this my sisters didn't know whether to laugh or cry themselves. But I could see that they were beginning to lose patience with a spoiled girl who expected to be treated as a goddess, and they were quite rightly beginning to let me know it.

I can see now that it was largely the shock of the change in life-style that was bothering me. Materially, there was not actually that much difference. Though I had lived in what is often called a palace, there had been no glass windows, no heating and no hot running water in Kumari Che, so winter was no more uncomfortable in my new life. The biggest difference was probably the crowding. As Kumari I had had my own room, but there was not enough room for this in the family house, so all five sisters slept in one room, Pramila and I in the bed, and the other three girls on mattresses on the floor. Perhaps if I had known what to say I could have joined in the conversations, but I always felt tongue-tied. I had never actually been expected to join in conversations as Kumari, though I could tell people what I wanted them to talk about.

If I was beginning to feel any affection for anyone, it was Pramila. My parents were still rather distant figures, and I felt awkward with them. Though I was poor at showing it, I felt more and more at home with my sisters, but it was natural to look up to Pramila, who was the oldest and the brilliant student. I still did not talk much to her, but would go to her with a comb and hand it to her, meaning that I wanted her to comb my hair. She was nice enough to do it for me. In the mornings, when she was hurrying to get ready for school, I used to ask her to choose a dress for me. After all, I had never had any choice before.

Since I had led such a sheltered life, and also because I had so little to do during the week, my father thought that it would be a good idea to introduce me to some of the sights of the valley, particularly the ones that were important to our Buddhist culture, so on Saturdays, his one day off, he would take us to places like Boudhanath, Gujeshwari or Swayambhunath.

At first I was very excited about these trips. Now I could go out once a week and be free instead of just being carried or pulled 13 times a year. It amazed me to be in a crowded bus with so many people all going in the same direction. Though I was a little frightened at first, my sisters told me to try to imagine I was in an especially big chariot pulled by many people. Then one day we were going to Gujeshwari near Pashupatinath. To the rest of the family it seemed like a short journey, but soon, as the bus swayed and the air got hotter and more fetid inside, I began to feel an uneasiness in my stomach that I had never experienced before. Luckily I was sitting by the window so I could see the view, because the next thing I knew, my breakfast came up all over the road. We were almost there by that time, so we got off and walked the rest of the way. "I don't like buses," I moaned weakly. "Let's walk home."

"It's part of life. You have to face it. You can't give up just because of one little incident," lectured Pramila, much to my irritation.

"Can't we walk home?" I pleaded. I had no idea of distances in those days.

"You can't go anywhere without getting on a bus sometimes," Pramila continued preaching.

My father, seeing how upset I had been by the experience interrupted. "We'll walk part of the way," he said. That became a pattern we followed (one time we walked half-way back from Dakshin Kali, which really is a long way). I wasn't happy at first about having to get on a bus at all, but for the first time I learned what a "compromise" was. I still don't like buses very much, but as Pramila said, you can't go anywhere without using them sometimes though luckily I can walk to my college classes.

In spite of the discomfort of the buses, the world was full of new experiences for me. I had known about sickness, but only from the outside, since so many people had come to pray for their sick children. What I had not really known about was poverty. Of course I had seen ragged urchins from the window of my palace, but they had been distant figures. Now I saw people all the time who were far less well off than we were, and at religious shrines I came face to face with the poorest of the poor who begged for their living. It helped me to realise how lucky I was, even though I was no longer a goddess.

Nor was I completely anonymous. My hair had always been thin, and the constant pulling it back into a tight bun during my years in Kumari Che had left me with two balding patches above the temples. Nepalis are people who are fond of speaking their minds, and it was not uncommon for someone on a bus to notice my bald spots and ask right out, "What's wrong with that girl? Has she been sick? Did she have typhoid?" Some victims of this disease lose their hair.

I never knew what to say, for I was still very shy in those days, so my father, or one of my sisters would explain that I had recently been the Royal Kumari. If the people who asked were Newari, or from the valley, they knew all about Kumari and many had seen me at one of the festivals. Outsiders and recent immigrants, however, needed a long explanation of just who, and what, Kumari was. Everyone seemed to realise that my divinity had passed to someone else, and no one on a bus ever tried to worship me.

During one of our early trips, at the great stupa of Boudhanath, we were walking around clockwise, the way all devotees do, when Pramila suddenly said to me, "You clomp."

"I what?"

"You clomp. Like a horse. You look silly, planting one foot down so firmly before you lift the other one up. Here, try to walk like me."

"I don't want to. I like the way I walk."

"But isn't it uncomfortable? And you can't keep up. We always have to wait for you. Especially since you insist on walking part of the way home."

"If I want to clomp, I'll clomp!" I shouted, bringing about a mild rebuke from my father.

"Now, now, Dyah Meiju," for they were still calling me that, "Let's not have any arguing in the family when we are all enjoying a nice day out." So I held my tongue, but I clomped more firmly than ever.

After one of these excursions we had gone to a cousin's house for dinner, and it was quite late when we were returning home. I was still clomping, and was concentrating on getting my feet in the right place, when I suddenly realised that we were in Durbar Square, right by Kashthamandap, and if we were in Durbar Square, then we could not be far from Kumari Che. I looked up and there it was, no more than fifty metres away.

Now, if I could just break away and run there before anyone knew what was happening. The whole family was talking away as usual, and seemed oblivious of me, so I took my chance, put my head down and made a dash for it.

If I was bad at walking, I was terrible at running, and almost as soon as I took off I could hear the laughter of my sisters. "She even runs like a horse," shouted my little brother. But I didn't care how I looked, as long as I got to the front door before anyone caught me. Without looking back I just kept running. Safe! I had made it. Except that the door was closed and bolted for the night. I pounded on it with all my might.

"Let me in! It's me! Oh hurry, before they take me away!" A surprised Gautam came to the door and let me in without comment. I rushed in, sure that someone would snatch me from behind.

In fact, I had no reason at all to worry. No one had followed me. My long-suffering family understood my unhappiness far better than I did myself, and though they must sometimes have been hurt by my behaviour, they were willing to let me find my own way. Instinctively, they knew it would be a long and difficult process.

"Let her go," someone must have said, once they had finished laughing at my comical run. "She can come to no harm there, and she'll come home when she is ready." In fact, I didn't come home for a week, then my mother came and got me. This time I did not try to refuse, nor did I complain.

It had been a good week, but I had begun to realise that there was no longer any sense in fighting. After all, at home I was surrounded by people who loved me and cared for me. They certainly did not mistreat me in any way, and even when they made fun of me, it was in the same careless and good-natured way that they made fun of one another. I was less and less a part of Kumari Che every time I went back. Someone had taken my place, and I was not really part of the caretaker family. Even a 12-year-old could see that. So I would try. I would try to be normal, to join in with the family banter, maybe even do my share of the housework. I was only hurting myself by behaving like I was. I knew it wouldn't be easy, in fact I knew I would have to be virtually reborn. But I also knew that the house was full of people who wanted nothing more than to help me.

1. The only photo of me before I was chosen as Kumari. I am second from right with my sisters.

2. The first photo of me as Kumari, at Ghoda-Jatra. This photo orginally appeared in the Royal Nepal Airlines magazine *Shangrila*.

3. The night before Indra Jatra. Another photo when I was very young. The garland on the naga indicates that this was the night of one of the two Nag Pujas (#35)

4. The Taleju Temple.

5. Kumari Che as it looked when I moved in. Before I left, the white facing was removed from the outer walls, restoring the building to its original appearance.

6. Being carried in front of Hanuman Dhoka for one of my smaller festivals.

7. With Maya and Laxmi at Seto Machendranath's bath.

8. Seto Machendranath being readied for his bath.

9. Seto Machendranath being repainted. I never actually saw this being done during my time as Kumari.

10. With my father the night before Indra Jatra.

11. Country women waiting for me to come out at Indra Jatra.

12. Ganesh peeking out the window of Kumari Che.

13. Walking to my chariot.

14. Being lifted up to my chariot.

15. Supporting my crown myself while everyone else is distracted.

16.

17. Indra's elephant.

18. Soldiers from Hanuman Dhoka in 18th century uniform.

19. Seto Bhairav. This image is only open during Indra Jatra.

20.

21. My first day home.

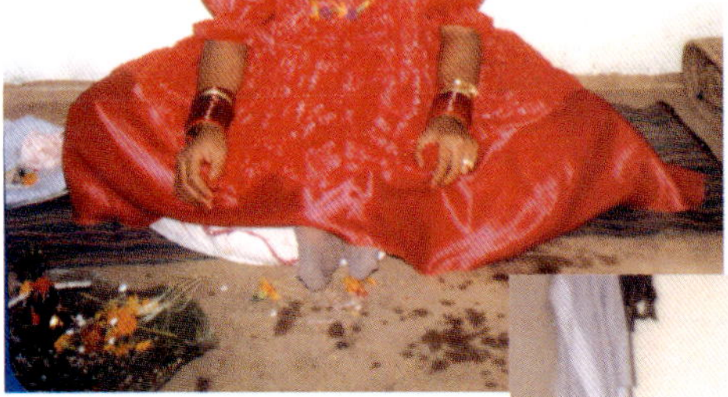

22. After changing my dress on my fourth day home.

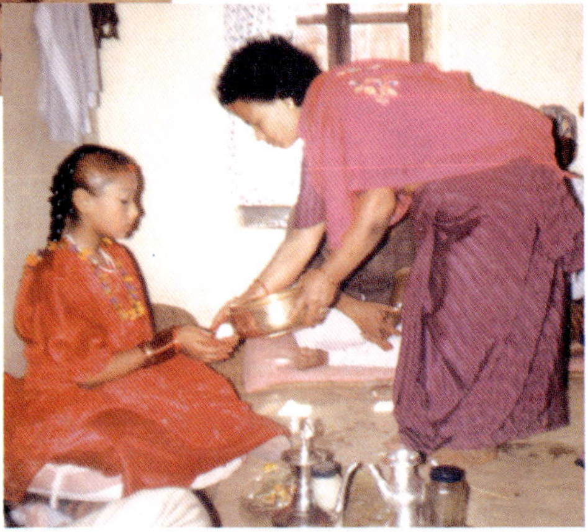

23. My fourth day home. Being offered *sagun* for the first time as myself rather than as a goddess.

25. One of the photos taken for the Independent article not long after my return. (Photo by Karen Willie)

24. With my mother, dressed up for my *ihi*, or bel fruit marriage.

26. Bahrah.

27. With my mother and friends, dressed up for Bahrah.

28. Me, right, in school uniform. Standing beside me is Samjhana. Sunila and my brother Sarbagya are seated.

29. All dressed up and made up for my disastrous CNN interview.

30. Dreaming. (Photo by Roberto Caccuri)

31. From goddess to mortal. (Photo by Surendra Puri)

32. A 2004 photo from the *Nepali Times* captioned: "Students find out about the internet at an Information Technology fair organised by Kantipur City College on Thursday." It was only by chance that I happened to be in the photograph. (Photo by Kiran Panday)

33. Launching, *Kathmandu Upatyakaka Kehi Sanskriti Chirka-Mirka* by Bhuwanlal Pradhan.

34. Coming out of Kumari Che for the function honouring former Kumaris.

35. With my mother on the same day.

36. Addressing the function honouring former Kumaris in Newari. The other seven former Kumaris are seated behind me and to my right.

37. With all the former Kumaris

38. Our mother with her six kids on Pramila's wedding day. I am in the back row behind my brother and next ro Pramila.

39. Welcoming a new brother to the family.

5

My sisters often complained that for the first two months I was home, I hardly spoke to them. After the first few days this was not so much because I was trying to distance myself from them, or that I wanted to be unfriendly, but mainly because I still felt shy. I was actually beginning to feel more and more comfortable with them, but their world was so different from mine that I just didn't know what to say to them. Have you ever felt that you would really like to talk with someone, but were just unable to make any words come out? That is how I felt, and not knowing what to do about it, I found it easiest to retreat into myself. Surmila, a year older than me, and the most outspoken, was not about to let me get away with it. "You can't go through life like this," she began scolding me almost as soon as I got home. "How are you going to learn to talk to the rest of the world if you won't even talk to us?" She put a lot of pressure on me to come out of my shell.

Pramila was now working for her Class 10 exam. This, the SLC or School Leaving Certificate, is the most important exam of any Nepali student's career, and she was often up very late till 12 or one o'clock, studying in the little pool of light created by her table lamp in the room we all shared. Long after Surmila had stopped trying to socialise me for the day and the other three girls had stopped chattering and joking around and had fallen asleep, I would lie awake watching Pramila. How could there possibly be so much to learn?

The light fascinated me. Since we were all in one room, Pramila would turn off the fluorescent light so as not to disturb the rest of us. In Kumari Che I had always slept in the dark by myself, whereas here I slept in the bed I shared with Pramila while my other sisters shared a mattress on the floor. Pramila was not the first person I had seen studying by the light of a table lamp. In Kumari Che, Mahendra Dai, my eldest "brother", had also studied like that. This made me curious, and I asked Pramila, "When will I be able to light the lamp?"

"What was that?" She looked up and smiled.

"When will I be able to study like you? When will I be able to light the lamp?"

To my surprise, she answered, "You don't have to be doing advanced studies to study with the table lamp. If you want to do this, all you have to do is start studying. If you want to start studying, then all you have to do is join the coaching class, and that starts soon. Do you want to study?"

I did, and she seemed to understand just how much I did. Though I didn't really know what coaching class was and what it would be like, I nodded my head in agreement.

It was the first conversation we had really shared. All our previous exchanges had been practical matters, like asking her to choose a dress for me, and even this was often done wordlessly.

In a big family, life becomes easier if everyone shares the burden. One custom we have in our family is that after meals everyone, from the smallest to the largest, washes his or her own dishes. It is not something that is actually forced on us, it is just that everyone, even my brother (and occasionally even my father) does it. It did not seem like a task to them, but everyone seemed to enjoy it. No one seemed to want to ask me to wash my own dishes, and I was shy of taking the first step. Sometimes I really wanted to, just to be more part of things, but I felt foolishly shy. Eventually, one evening I just picked up my plate and washed it and continued to do it after that.

Though I had resolved to change myself after the time I ran away, in fact I wasn't sure how to go about it, and my family were still worried that I intended to spend the rest of my life sitting around. I'm not sure whose idea it was, but to show me what my life might be like, I was taken to visit a previous Kumari who stayed at home doing pretty much what I was now doing: nothing.

I was left there in the morning. Though we both had names, we were both also Dyah Meiju, so we didn't know how to address one another. She did not seem interested in talking to me anyway. The main feature of her room was a large mirror, and she had lots of bottles of make-up and nail polish. It was with these that she busied herself for most of the day.

When I got home, my sisters asked me how I had enjoyed my day. "I didn't," I said, for once anxious to talk with them. "I was bored stiff."

"What did you talk about?" asked Surmila.

"Nothing. We didn't talk at all."

"Well then, what did you do all day?" asked Samjhana.

"I didn't do anything. She just sat in front of the mirror and put on make-up."

"Boring," commented my little brother.

"That's what I said."

"Why wasn't she in school?" asked Sunila, the youngest sister. "She should be in college by now."

"She never really went to school," answered Pramila. "Only for a short time. Then she said she didn't like it, and no one insisted."

"Everyone still calls her Dyah Meiju," I said. Everyone still called *me* Dyah Meiju, but when I saw it happening to a young woman of her age, it did not seem right. I knew it would have to stop sometime. "Her grandmother seems very proud of her, and doesn't make her do anything. She brought us lunch and after we ate I was going to wash my plates like I do at home, but she stopped me. She said Dyah Meiju never does anything like that."

"Her life isn't much like ours, is it?" commented Pramila.

"It sure isn't" I agreed. "You are all so busy. She doesn't have anything to do but look at herself all day."

"Which life do you think you would like?" asked Surmila. They all knew the answer. I don't know why anyone wanted me to say it. When I remained silent, she said. "You'll see. You'll enjoy coaching class."

I wasn't sure. But before coaching class began, there was time to catch up on an important little ceremony. In order to qualify as Kumari it was necessary that I had not gone through the *ihi* ceremony which most Newari girls do when they are very young. It is normally a group activity in which girls from a community are symbolically married to a bel fruit, and because it is done in a large group, it is usually an important occasion for a young girl. In my case, I had to do it by myself since we could not wait until the time for a group ceremony, and in any case participating in a group ceremony is very expensive. The only temple that does the ceremony for individuals is Bijeshwori, just north-west of the city on the far side of the Vishnumati River. My mother, my father's elder sister and I went by taxi. Bijeshwori, enshrining the Akash Yogini, is one of the most powerful temples in the valley, but I was unaware of this at the time. Though I was again dressed in red, I did not feel like Kumari anymore, and the whole ceremony for some reason left me unimpressed except for the novelty of doing puja to a goddess instead of having it done to me. At any rate, I was now married to the dried fruit that would never disintegrate, and whatever else might happen, I would never be a widow.

In Kathmandu schools have a 2-month winter vacation, but this does not mean that all children get to have two months off. There were special coaching classes for weak students, and others for students like Pramila who were about to take an important exam. It was decided that coaching class would be my first experience of formal education. The class was only two hours, and I would not have to wear a uniform, so that this would be a good way to ease me into something new. I had wanted to go to school since those days of wandering around Kumari Che by myself looking into the classrooms of the school next door, and now would be my chance.

But would coaching class suit me? I was not a weak student, I was no student at all. I was supposed to know everything, but in fact I knew nothing. This could be embarrassing. But I had seen how one of my predecessors lived. It looked a lot better to work towards "lighting the lamp", and this was the first step.

But first I had to get myself there. While I had never had any trouble getting up in the morning (and in a room with four sisters rushing around getting ready for school, it would have been impossible to sleep in anyway), I was not accustomed to having to be in a certain place at a given time, and the idea that I had to leave the house no later than a specific time was difficult to relate to. Even my festivals hadn't started until everyone was ready, and at first I just couldn't understand what the hurry was all about, especially since during winter vacation it was only Pramila and me who had to go. Since I wouldn't be wearing a uniform I had to choose a dress. I usually asked Pramila to do this for me, but on the first day it was easy. It was cold outside, so I chose the green one because it was the warmest.

It was about a ten minute walk to the school, but I didn't know that yet since it was my first day. The whole way I badgered Pramila with questions. How far was the school? How many subjects would I have to learn? What were the teachers like? I wasn't nervous, but I was excited.

When we got to the school, Pramila showed me my room, then went off to her own class. I found myself in a classroom, for the first time ... with about fifteen other children who were about half my size. They were all about five or six years old, and I stood out as much as if I had been wearing my Indra Jatra clothes. The teacher came in, the only one in the room who was bigger than I was, and we all sat down. Then she asked each of us our names. I wasn't sure what to say, and mumbled "Kumari".

The class was for two hours, and on that day we did English spelling, Nepali and a little of what is "science" to five-year-olds: things like the names of flowers and animals. Since the students were the slowest ones, of course everything was conducted on a very basic level. The Nepali alphabet was easy for me since it was one of the few things that my teacher had insisted on me learning. But the English alphabet really stumped me. I could recognise only the capital letters and could write them beautifully, but I was confused over what the sounds attached to them were.

The two hours passed quickly, and my mind was exhausted at the end of it. But it had been fun. It was a little strange sitting with children so small, but no one bullied me or made fun of me. "Namaste, Kumari Didi,"[1] several of them said to me, their hands folded and big smiles on their little faces. I replied with my own Namaste, and met Pramila at the gate.

"How was it?" she asked.

I thought for a moment before I answered. "I think I'm going to like it."

"What was the teacher's name?"

I couldn't remember anything about her except that she was rather stout. "Moti Miss," I replied, and we both laughed. "Moti" means "fat" in Nepali. She asked about the other kids and seemed relieved that no one had made fun of me for being behind.

At home everyone was curious as to how my morning had gone. It was a strange feeling to be the busy one while the others had a holiday. I found myself talking and answering their questions, and did not even notice that I was almost behaving like one of the family.

In the afternoon I proudly worked on my homework. I had to write the names of ten colours, ten animals and ten flowers, all in English. Considering that my teacher in Kumari Che had never

---

[1] *Didi* is Nepali for "elder sister"

taught me anything but the capital letters, I thought I did pretty well to write out things like "BLUE", "WHITE", and "RED". I managed about five colours, then kept running after my sisters asking for more. They couldn't imagine that I had gone through life without knowing "purple". There were some multiplication problems as well, but they were easy for me since I had already memorised the times tables up to 22, and was accustomed to doing multiplication problems of four digits by four digits.

As the days went on I began to see that there were things that came easily to me and others that did not. English was always a problem, especially pronunciation. Science was new to me as well, even at the basic level we were studying, and while I could multiply with ease, I had trouble relating the numbers to a problem like, "If one mango costs 2 rupees, how much do two mangoes cost?" But I soon figured out that I had a house full of sisters who could help me. When I had a problem with my homework, I would just approach one of them with my notebook and ask her. They were always happy to help me, but I did not realise that sometimes they laughed at me behind my back, not because they thought I was stupid, but because they found me very cunning in getting answers out of them.

One day as we walked to school, we found one of my classmates waiting for me. She obviously wanted to be friendly, and Pramila walked behind so we could talk. In fact I didn't enjoy her chatter very much, because she spent most of the time criticising my poor English. "You don't even know *that* much spelling?" she asked derisively after I had got a zero in dictation. It was very difficult for me to take criticism or ridicule because this was the first time I had ever had a friend I could not order around.

For the first two or three weeks, the teachers continued to call me "Kumari". However, this seemed a little awkward since I was not really Kumari anymore, and one day one of the teachers called on "Rashmila" to answer a question. At first I was so surprised that I didn't answer, but I quickly recovered. Then I was anxious for her to call on me again. When I heard my name the next time, I answered right up. It was fun, a kind of a novelty, like being someone else. It was also the first time that anyone had used my name since I was too young to remember.

At home I was still Dyah Meiju, but my sisters were becoming a little uncomfortable with it. When it came time to register me for normal classes, I was registered as Rashmila Shakya, not as "Kumari" or "Dyah Meiju".

I progressed in coaching class until I felt ready and even anxious for real school to begin. Though I had never before had to discipline myself and concentrate for as long as 2 hours (except during some of the festivals, and then all I had had to do was sit), I did not find the 2-hour coaching classes difficult, and I felt prepared for a new challenge, wearing a school uniform and carrying a bag just like a real student.

* * * *

"Rashmila, hurry up. We'll all be late for school!"

This was something new again. One of my sisters was calling me, using my name rather than Dyah Meiju. It was the first morning of school, and everything was to be different.

"Rashmila, what are you doing? We'll have to leave without you!"

Well, I had hurried, and I was nearly ready, but an unforeseen problem had come up. Wearing the uniform was something I had looked forward to, and I felt grown up as I put on the blue shirt, the silly tie and the hair ribbon that matched the shirt. But I had never looked at the length of the navy blue skirt. It only came down to my knees! All my life I had worn skirts that came down to my ankles, and now people, boys even, were going to see my legs. What could I do? I thought of climbing back into bed and claiming to be sick, but I knew everyone would see through this.

Besides, I wanted to go to school, and I wanted to hear people calling me Rashmila.

So I did the only thing I could think of and pulled up my navy blue socks, stretched them as far as I could until they came right up to my knees. It wasn't perfect, but it was the best I could do. I grabbed my bag and went down the steep stairs as quickly as I could.

And now another problem arose that I hadn't thought of, as I looked at my new school shoes. They were made of leather. As Kumari I had never been allowed to wear anything made of leather, or even to touch anyone wearing leather.

"What's wrong?" asked Sunila who was 6 years old and would be my class-mate.

"Nothing," I answered, gritted my teeth, and put on my shoes. Not only were they leather, but they were new, and they hurt. Just when I was getting this walking on the street business down and not clomping anymore, my school shoes made me feel like I would have to learn to walk all over again.

"Hurry up Rashmila. Why are you dawdling? We're already late." I didn't answer, but just concentrated on walking in my painful new shoes. The more they insisted, the more nervous I became, and the more difficult it was to keep up. We finally reached the school.

"Fifteen minutes instead of the usual ten," commented someone. "We're going to have to leave earlier if this keeps up." It wasn't the most auspicious start to my scholarly career.

By now, although I was getting used to being with children much smaller than I was, it was a shock seeing so many of them—there were about forty in a regular class—and all in identical uniforms. I was excited about this first day of school, but seeing so many little children almost made me want to turn around and go home. What was a novelty was having my youngest sister in the same class. She seemed quite proud to have her big sister as a classmate, and a little protective as well. But she needn't have worried. I already knew some of the kids from coaching class, and though everyone else was calling me Rashmila now, they still called me Kumari Didi. Even so, Sunila sat next to me in the next to back row, just in case I was nervous.

Sunila was not the only thing that was familiar about the class, because Pramila had been hired as a part-time teacher while she awaited the results of her SLC exam. She took the first period. English composition. Ugh. My worst subject. It was good having a familiar face, though she did not obviously favour me. Several other of her friends were also working part-time at the school, and so I knew a lot of my teachers.

It was a long day for me, from 9:30 to 4, by far the longest time I had ever had to do anything. But though I was tired, I was still excited and full of questions as I limped and clomped my way home.

"Slow down," I called, as I tried to catch up. "I want to ask you about my books."

"Keep up with us and you can ask all you want."

I did my best. "What's this one? What does 'guided' mean?" I called out, hoping someone would take the trouble to answer because my "Guided English" book looked really scary, full of long, difficult reading passages.

There was not as much time to do my homework as when I had been to coaching class, and it was more difficult as well. The word problems were beginning to make more sense ("You have 7 apples, and you give three to a friend. How many are left?"), but English was still a problem. We had been given a dictation in class. As always, I had made a mess of it, and I had to correct my spelling. Luckily I had Pramila to ask about the pronunciation, because I hadn't got a clue.

Going to school made me feel more a member of the family, even if I was so far behind. Now I was no longer sitting around wondering what to do with myself while everyone else was so busy. I was doing just what everyone else was, and driving my sisters crazy asking for help with my homework, for I was very anxious not to fall behind, or fail. Just how distinct a possibility that was, was brought home to me one day by my little brother, still my favourite of the family, and now a year behind me in Class 1. One day he said: "You are studying with Sunila now. Why don't you fail? Then you can study with me!" He was only joking and meant no harm, but it did make me think, and made me more determined than ever to succeed.

I was growing up and becoming more independent in other ways as well. My father had given me some spending money, and one day I felt like some chocolate, so I told my mother I was going out to buy some. Then I walked apprehensively across the road to a small shop and bought 25 rupees worth of Dairy Milk chocolates. It might seem like a small thing, or something of no significance, but it was a big step for me. For the first time I handled money by myself. Of course I knew in theory that people gave money to shop-keepers and got things in return, but knowing about something and actually doing it are two different things. I was surprised at how much chocolate you got for 25 rupees, and there was plenty to share with my sisters. I was very proud of myself. On the other hand, it seemed a strange thing to have to do. Before, chocolates had always been offered to me. It had never occurred to me that I might have to go to so much effort just to get some.

Luckily I had had some experience of cooking when I was still Kumari since once I got home I could no longer just order people around. One day when I wanted a snack I just went up to the kitchen[1] and made an omelette and tea for myself. It should have occurred to me to clean up as well, but I'm afraid I left that for my mother. I still had a few things to learn.

Now that I was doing more of the things my sisters were doing, I began to feel more comfortable sitting with the family at

---

[1] Newari kitchens are traditionally on the top floor of the house.

meals. Since I had always eaten my main meals by myself ever since I could remember, it had been difficult for me to sit with others, though it had seemed natural enough to sit with the family in Kumari Che on my visits. For the first few months at home I used to sit to one side and just let them talk, though they sometimes got on my nerves so much with their chatter that I asked them to be quiet. As the months passed, I enjoyed listening to their talk more and more as it began to make more sense to me. But after school started there seemed no sense in sitting by myself, and soon found myself able to join in, though I still felt shy about addressing my parents. In fact, I did not call them "Father" and "Mother" for a long time. But that was not out of disrespect or dislike, but because I had never called *anyone* Father and Mother that I could remember. I know it upset my mother, and I sometimes wonder how she put up with me during that first year or two.

But while I was learning to relate to the family, I was still shy with outsiders. "You just shut up completely when anyone else is around," Surmila would complain. "Especially boys."

"Why should I talk with boys?"

"Because they are half the world, that's why, and if you just sit there and act dumb, they will walk all over you."

One time a boy cousin was visiting, and when he tried to talk to me, as usual I just sat silently looking at the floor. "Does Dyah Meiju think she is too good to talk to her humble relatives?" he asked, at once making fun of me and addressing me as goddess. I felt myself turn red, but no words would come out.

"You leave her alone!" Surmila shot back at him. "If you want to pick on someone, pick on me." But I could tell that I was the one she was angry at, and after he had gone she gave me a good scolding.

"You can't go on like this. First of all, you are not Dyah Meiju anymore. And second, you have to learn to stand up for yourself.

Don't let guys get away with stuff like that! Be proud that you are a woman and don't let guys humiliate you!"

It did not take me long to realise that while my parents still respected me as a former goddess, I could not order them around the way I had my family at Kumari Che. They might have accepted it, but my sisters never would have. I was still as fond of tomato *achar* as ever, and realising that I could no longer get away with mini hunger strikes, I began to keep track of how much was left. Two days before it would run out I would tell my father, who is much better at bargaining and so does most of the family shopping, so that he could buy tomatoes on his way home and my mother could pickle them.

Not all my new experiences, as I learned to relate to the world at large, were pleasant. During the first week of school, I wanted to put covers on my textbooks and exercise books. Looking around for something to use, I saw a magazine full of colourful pictures in the front room. It was just what I wanted, so I began to pull out the pages, fold them around the books and scotch tape them on. It took me some time because I was still a little awkward and clumsy, but when I was finished I was quite proud of myself.

I went to find someone to show off my accomplishment to and saw Pramila looking around for something. She was looking everywhere: under cushions, under furniture, everywhere. When she saw me, she did not even greet me but just asked if I had seen her *Newsweek*.

"What's a *Newsweek*?" I asked.

"It's a magazine I buy every week. I've been looking forward to reading it."

"No, Didi, I haven't seen it. But look what I've done." I proudly showed her my newly covered exercise books and textbooks.

"But ... but, you've covered your books with my *Newsweek*!" She looked more upset than I had ever seen her look before.

"They were just colourful pictures. I ... I liked the colours."

"70 rupees! That's how much *Newsweek* costs. 70 rupees! It is my big treat of the week!"

"Well ... I'll, I'll buy you another one."

"Ha! Where will *you* get 70 rupees? People don't throw money at you anymore! Oh you stupid, *stupid* girl!"

And then she hit me. On the back, not very hard, and not really as if to hurt me, but nevertheless she actually hit a former Kumari.

No one had ever hit me, even in fun, and no one had ever spoken to me so angrily. I think we were both a little shocked and just stood looking at one another. I was close to tears, but was determined not to let on. I understood that I had done something wrong, but I really had not known at the time.

And Pramila understood that as well when she had had a moment to calm down, for eventually she gave me a fond smile. "Oh well, there's always next week. And we can't expect you to learn everything right away." And in fact, it was all for the best. My other sisters were always getting into little fights and occasionally bashing each other. In the end, this disagreement only served to make me feel more a member of the real world.

It took me about a week to get used to my short skirt and leather shoes, and to sitting in a classroom full of such small children. One thing I could not get used to, though, was going outside to play with them during recess period. They were just too small to be interesting. And so I just sat at my desk while they went outside. My teacher, not quite sure what to do about this, ordered me outside, but I refused to go. Eventually we negotiated through Pramila and I was allowed to stay inside. I would just sit by the window and watch the smaller kids play.

It was not that I disliked the children. They were like little brothers and sisters to me, and they were full of questions.

"Kumari Didi, how did you become a goddess?" they would ask during break times, and I would tell them about the *battis lagchan* and my horoscope and about my meeting with the king that I did not remember.

"Kumari Didi, how did you feel being a goddess?" And I told them about how nice it had been being the centre of attention, having people pray to me and throw offerings like flowers, rice and coins at me during festivals, and how once I had my naga necklace on I didn't feel like talking to anyone, or smiling.

"Kumari Didi, is it true that you are the most beautiful girl in Kathmandu?" How was I supposed to answer that one?

"Kumari Didi, is it true that no man will marry you because he will die young?" That is the only question that I refused to answer. Even when I got sick of answering the same things over and over again, I tried to be polite. But this was not even a very nice thing to think about, and besides, I was 12 years old. It is still not a question I am particularly fond of.

As the weeks went by, I became so busy that, without even realising it, I began to lose my homesickness. I quickly got used to getting up with my sisters and going out to the small nearby Ganesh and Saraswati shrines for an early morning puja before breakfast.[1] The rest of the day soon settled into busy routine. It was a routine that was not without worries, however, as I began to wonder if I would pass my exams. This is the first time I ever remember worrying about anything in my life.

I was not the only one to worry. My parents were happy that I was going to school, and trying to be normal, but they were concerned that I was so far behind, especially in English, and wondered how I would ever catch up. Our neighbours, who saw me leaving for school every morning with my sisters, were curious about how I was doing and if I would be able to continue since they had never heard of an ex-Kumari going to school. To

---

[1] Elephant-headed Ganesh is a favourite with Newari Buddhists as well as Hindus while Saraswati, goddess of education and art, is to us another name for Manjushree.

their credit, they never criticised the decision to send me to school. This was in contrast to some of our more conservative relatives who felt that it was wrong to make a former goddess struggle or work hard.

In fact, we received some rather strong criticism from relatives who saw me washing dishes, or washing and ironing my own clothes. Everyday chores like this were an adventure for me, and I enjoyed them, but sometimes when they told me I was not a normal girl and that Dyah Meiju should not be doing such things, I wondered just what was correct. It was at times like this that Pramila or Surmila would remind me of the Nepali folk story in one of my Nepali textbooks of "The Father, the Son and the Donkey". It begins with all three of them walking, and people saying that the father and son are stupid because although they have a donkey neither of them is riding. So hearing that they both get on the donkey, but after a little while the people around say, "Poor donkey, carrying two people." So the father gets off, but after they have gone a little further the people say, "Poor father. Though he is old he has to walk. Very naughty son." So the son gets off and the father rides. But the people still feel sorry for the donkey. Then they tie the donkey's feet to a pole so they can carry him. But as they are crossing a bridge, the donkey moves around and they drop him in the river. The moral of the story is don't always be changing your mind according to what other people say. And my sisters were right. If I had listened to the wrong people, I would have wound up thoroughly bored.

Before I had started school, I had done my *ihi* ceremony years late. About 6 months later, it was time for the second mock marriage ritual we do called *bahrah*, or *gufa*, which means "cave". This is even more of a growing up ceremony than *ihi*, and one we have to do before our first period. After it we are supposed to be grown up, and in fact a common way of scolding an older girl is to remind her that she "has been given *gufa*", and so should not be acting like a child anymore.

The time for doing it was given to us by a priest who had studied my horoscope. Four girls did it together, two of our neighbours as well as Sunila and me. Again I was the biggest. But I thoroughly enjoyed it. For 12 days we were kept in a "dark" room. In fact, it is not actually dark, but the sun is not allowed in. During that time no men or boys, not even our fathers or brothers, are allowed to see us. We were not allowed to eat meat, *dal* or eggs, but had no responsibilities, and spent our time playing. There was also a little demon or ghost present called the *Bahrah Kyhah*. Some castes make a little cloth image of him, but we only leave an empty place for him. At night we used to frighten one another by making noises and saying the *Bahrah Kyhah* was coming to get us. With the isolation and the playmates, it was a little like living in Kumari Che again, although one difference was that there was a maths exam at the time, and Pramila brought it so that Sunila and I could take it.

On the twelfth day, when we came out, we were dressed like brides in red with full make-up, but our faces were covered because we were not allowed to see the sun until we had done a puja. When we were taken to the roof, we first saw the reflection of the sun in a basin of water. After that we did something called giving *aradi*, or giving light to the sun. This was followed by a puja to a stone carving of the sun, after which we were taken downstairs to do a puja to a mandala symbolising the universe. At the end of all this, we were considered married to Surya, the god of the sun.

In the end, I didn't feel as if I had passed a threshold or was more grown up; I just felt like I had had a really nice time. I was not unusual in this. Most of the girls I know seem to feel this way, but our parents certainly regard us as being more grown up, and expect us to behave accordingly.

Though I was leaving my former life as Kumari further behind, I did not divorce myself from it entirely. I still continued my visits to Kumari Che, and was officially invited to all the festivals in which I had previously participated. The first one I went to was Seto Machendranath Jatra, the one where the chariot had seldom turned up during my 8 years. It was a strange feeling, seeing another girl sitting in my place, much stranger than having her living in my room at Kumari Che. On the other hand, it was so interesting to watch the festival from the outside as one of the crowd that I wasn't at all jealous of her.

I had much the same feeling at Seto Machendranath's bath, but at the first Indra Jatra I attended, I felt positively relieved to be on the outside looking in. When I had been the centre of attention, it had seemed normal, and I didn't realise until I saw it as an observer just how strongly I had felt my responsibilities. Now, for the first time, I could actually relax and enjoy the festivals. It was amazing watching the big chariot being pulled by so many young guys. And at Godha Jatra, the horse festival, I not only got to watch the Kumari procession for the first time, but not being stuck in the RNAC building behind a tree, I actually got to see what was going on.

At some time during this period, we were first approached by a journalist, from the British newspaper *The Independent*, for an interview. The article appeared in March, 1992, so the interview must have taken place about the time I was doing coaching class, or just starting regular school. In fact, I have no remembrance of the interview, but Pramila remembers it well, because it was the first time she had been interviewed in English, and she was very nervous. It is hard to imagine her nervous about anything, but she was only 16. Since he had just turned up unannounced, Pramila did not know what to do with him, didn't let him in the house, and conducted the interview in the courtyard. I certainly couldn't have made much of an impression since he wrote that "...the trauma of having been a *kumari* was evident ..." The photographer took some nice black and white pictures of me though, in which I think I look more contented than traumatised.

These were early days for us as far as the media was concerned, and Pramila was happy to have survived the interview at all. I was only a small part of the article which concentrated mostly on Nani Maya Shakya who had been Kumari in the late 60s and early 70s, had later passed her School Leaving Certificate, married, had several children and opened a pharmacy. We were pleased that we were sent the article, and we were all excited to see my photo, as ex-Kumari, in a foreign newspaper. On the other hand, the article repeated uncritically the marriage legend as well as the "nightmarish examination" of the 108 buffalo and goat heads as part of the selection process. He quoted Nani Maya as saying she remembered this, but I think he probably misunderstood when she spoke of later memories of Kal Ratri. We have also learned since that Nepali interpreters tend to be a bit imaginative, and since they often do not know very much about the Kumari tradition themselves, they often tell foreign journalists what they want to hear.

Later, when we had more experience with journalists, we would always try to emphasise several things with them. First and foremost was that the legend of trying to scare little girls with 108 freshly severed buffalo and goat heads was untrue. Even on Kal Ratri, as I remember it, there were only about a dozen heads, and the puja was solemn rather than frightening. Next was that it was untrue that a Kumari is automatically de-selected if she ever bleeds or cries. As you have seen, I had unexplained crying fits during 1990 that were thought to be related to the democracy movement and the loss of power by the king. And third was that vexed question of marriage.

Though we never actually ask for anything in return for granting an interview except for a copy of the article, foreign journalists have often offered to compensate us for our time, calling this, logically enough, a donation towards my educational expenses. Most journalists have also been courteous enough to send us copies of their published articles.

Once the first few difficult months were over, my first year in the real world passed quickly because I was so busy. Partially because I was older and could concentrate more, and partially because I was so determined, I had no problems with my school subjects except English, which would always remain a problem. The 27% I got in English Composition in the first term was nothing to brag about. And then there was the 17% in General Knowledge. Well, what could they expect? Besides, everyone did poorly in that subject after a new teacher mistakenly set the wrong questions. My first semester conduct was only "Fair", but after that I settled down. And the 79% in mathematics was a herald of things to come and helped bring my overall average up to 60.7%. In the end, I think the comment I got for the final semester, "She has done very well. Try to keep up like this," was more than just empty encouragement.

As the year went on, the principal suggested that I skip Class 3 and be promoted straight to Class 4. At least I had outsmarted my little brother. The principal knew it would be a little difficult for me, but with Pramila working as a part-time teacher and with the rest of my family as students at the same school, she knew that I could count on a lot of help. There was no sense, she felt, in letting me just do a year at a time, or I would be 22 before I reached Class 10 and sat for my SLC. And so it was decided that I would do my best to go through two grades every year until I was caught up. I was all for it, because the quicker I progressed, the sooner I would be with kids my own age. I had a lot of hard work ahead of me.

6

For the benefit of non-Nepali readers, this would be a good time to step back and explain how the educational system here works. Generally the students start their school life from kindergarten at the age of 3 or 4. They have 3 years in kindergarten: nursery, junior and senior. I had completed only nursery class and was in junior when I was chosen to be Kumari. After kindergarten, students join Grade 1 (or Class 1, as we often call it) and continue to Grade 10 when they take the SLC or School Leaving Certificate, generally around the age of 16 or 17. As mentioned previously, this is the most important exam of any Nepali student's life, and is roughly equivalent to the British GCSE, though there is nothing really similar in the American system.

The results of the SLC determine what a student will do next in life. Those who do well go to University Colleges for one of two courses: either Plus 2 or for the more scientifically inclined, ISC (Intermediate Science Certificate). These are roughly equivalent to British "A" levels, or the International Baccalaureate, and are probably a little more advanced than the average American High School Diploma. The top students in Plus 2 and ISC will qualify for government universities, which are free. Those who have done less well, but who still want to further their education, can go to private universities if their families can afford it, or if they can qualify for a scholarship.

Since I had only completed one year of kindergarten, technically, I should not even have been allowed into Class 1. However, since all my sisters and my brother were studying at the same private school and the principal was happy with them, I had been allowed into Class 2 on the condition that I be given extra tuition at home.

I should also explain that since the government of Nepal struggles to provide enough places in its schools, there are a great many inexpensive, English-medium, private schools in Nepal. Private education is not only for the wealthy or privileged as in some countries, and a surprising number of children go to private schools, especially in the urban centres. In fact, I got in without having to pay the fees since the school had a policy of letting one sibling in for free for every three fee-paying ones, and our family had not yet used its quota. At this point I also had a "pension" of 300 rupees (the equivalent of about 6 US dollars) a month which would continue until my 22nd birthday. It just went into the kitty, and was helpful with the expenses of a large family. At least I was not a financial burden.

So now I was 13 and in Class 4. The other students were only about 4 years younger than I was now, and the biggest girl in the class, who was about my size, became my best friend. Since I had left my former classmates behind, I was no longer "Kumari Didi" to anyone, but just plain Rashmila. On the other hand, everyone knew that I had been Kumari, and I was still occasionally asked questions about my old life (the same questions all the time, it seemed), which I was now well-accustomed to answering. During this year, my shyness about playing with the other children also left me, and I began to feel a little more comfortable with them even though they were still so much younger.

While I was in Class 2 or 4, though I don't actually remember it, the father of the new Kumari, whom my family had met for the first time at the handing-over ceremony, came to visit us. He was already concerned about what would happen to his daughter in seven or eight years, and he had come to ask how I was doing. My parents answered honestly that after the first few months at home I was adjusting well socially, but that I was way behind in school and would have to work hard to catch up. On the basis of what they told him, he petitioned the government to provide more complete and useful lessons for his daughter. He was eventually successful, though not before his petition had been handed to the King Birendra himself during Indra Jatra, and soon the Kumari began having not the desultory hour-a-day I had had, but three hours private tuition from teachers at the school she would be attending at the end of her term of office. The idea was that when she finished she would be able to go straight into Class 6 or 7 with children of her own age. This was quite a revolutionary change in the way Royal Kumaris were to be educated, and I am proud that my family and I had a hand in bringing it about.

I think it was when I was in Class 2 that another Kumari article appeared in the popular international women's magazine, *Elle*. I was not interviewed for this, nor were we sent a copy of the article, though friends later gave us one. I assume I was not sent a copy of the article because the author had no idea who I was. In it the Kumari who took office in the year 1984 (that was the year I became Kumari) was identified as "Prem Sobha Shakya". Then there was a photograph which was supposedly her, but which in fact was the Bhaktapur Ekanta Kumari. While I do know of a woman named Prem Sobha Shakya, she is the daughter of a former Kumari, and her mother specifically refused to let her be considered as Kumari. The article also repeated the standard tale of the buffalo heads and the "intimate physical examination". My family and I were beginning to learn that journalists often do not do their homework, and are likely to come out with the most remarkable drivel.

It is hardly surprising that my memories of the next three years are rather vague. I must have been extremely busy. Apparently I bugged my sisters constantly for help. Surmila was in Class 10 when I was in Class 4, and was so busy studying for her SLC that she could be of very little assistance to me, so as usual most of the burden fell on Pramila. But after all, one of the conditions of my skipping grades was that I get plenty of help and encouragement at home.

I also remember an argument I had with my mother at the time. She was busy doing something and had asked me to make tea. As usual, I was very slow. It wasn't that I purposely dawdled, but I was still learning to do the things my sisters had picked up as a matter of course much younger. Always one to speak her mind, my mother scolded me, "Why can't you be more like your sisters? It doesn't take that long to make tea. And you don't have any friends either," she added just for good measure. "Why don't you chat with people, learn how to talk and make friends?"

"If you wanted me to be like that, then why did you let me be Kumari in the first place?" I shot back, angry. For once she was at a loss for words.

This exchange was reported in a 1994 article in *Cosmopolitan* entitled "I was a Goddess". Western women's magazines seemed to be fond of publishing Kumari articles. My mother was interviewed for this article, and while she is more or less fairly reported, it should be remembered that at the time she was interviewed I was still going through a difficult period. As my mother remembers it, the interview took place during my *bahrah* confinement, during that first year home when I was confused and having a particularly difficult time relating to my parents. She is quoted as saying, "If I had known then what I know now, I never would have let her become Kumari." This is a fair enough reflection of how she felt at the time, but she now feels that the recent changes in the education policy might cause her to feel differently.

But while the parts of the article concerning me and my family were fair and balanced, the rest of the article was really shocking. There are some nice photographs, but their captions are completely wrong. This article continues the tradition of publishing photos of one of the more accessible of the valley's

Kumaris (Patan, Bhaktapur or Bungamati) and calling them the Royal Kumari. There is even one of Ganesh or Bhairav at Indra Jatra with the implication that it is Kumari. A photo captioned "Kumari candidates await screening by priests and the royal astrologer" is actually a photo of girls dressed up for an *ihi* ceremony. Kumari candidates would not get together like that or dress like that, and once you have done *ihi* you are not eligible anyway. The business about a Kumari candidate witnessing the sacrifice of 108 buffaloes and goats is even in garish purple and white print by the pictures. It is even claimed that the girl has to "walk anti-clockwise over the animals' freshly severed heads."

There is one paragraph in particular in which there is not a single correct statement. It is claimed that a Kumari has no companions but priests and has to spend a long time every morning doing puja. It goes on to insist that the girl is kept illiterate, has a "strict" diet and is even kept in ignorance about her previous life with her family. Furthermore, she is supposedly forbidden from both laughing and crying. She even has to walk on white cloths inside Kumari Che, and can never go out in the sun. The paragraph concludes that, "The silk hung rooms she lives in are her prison."

There are also words attributed to me ("When I began to menstruate, I did not know what was happening.") that I could not possibly have said at that age. Sometimes I find this sort of thing laughable, but it can be offensive as well. I have often wished that foreign journalists and editors would stop trying to play up the spectacular and look a little bit harder for the truth.

Back at school, it was important to me that I should get the best results possible and catch up. I was always either doing my homework or chasing my sisters around asking for help. I suppose you could say that, except in matters like making cups of tea in a reasonable amount of time, I was developing a sense of responsibility. So much so that during these years my studies became more important to me than attending some of the old

Kumari festivals. Former Kumaris are always invited to attend the big festivals, especially Indra Jatra, but it is not compulsary that they attend. My second semester exams sometimes fell during Indra Jatra, and since my school work was the most important thing for me, I began missing the biggest Kumari festival of the year for the sake of my studies.

Perhaps my report cards for those years tell the story better than my scant memories. On the cover of my Class 4 report card, in Surmila's handwriting, is written "Kumari" in pencil, and under it "Who?" My marks were not spectacularly good, though I did manage 65 in English Composition. An average of 61.1 was enough to get me promoted past Class 5 to Class 6. In the Nepali system, marking is quite tough, with passing at 40%, and 60% considered quite a good mark. I might have been feeling a bit stretched in Class 6, since my average slumped to 57.8. I failed two English Composition exams and wound up with an overall mark in English Composition of 45. Even in maths I only managed 61.5. Teachers' comments emphasised that I had to work hard in English Composition.

At this point it was decided that I had skipped as many grades as was feasible, so the next year I went from Class 6 into Class 7. This was the year of my little brother's *bare chuyegu* ceremony, a ceremony done by all Bajracharya and Shakya boys when they become monks for four days, and harks back to the time when our *baha*, were actual monasteries inhabited by celibate monks. All Shakya men are members of a *baha*, which they officially join during this ceremony. It might be remembered that my father had to be a member of one of the central Kathmandu *baha* for me to be considered as Kumari.

Bare chuyegu is the boys' equivalent of the *ihi* and *bahrah* ceremonies that we girls have to go through, and like them is a growing up ceremony. Except as a participant in my own *ihi* and *bahrah* ceremonies, this was the first function of this sort I had attended and I really enjoyed the social occasion with all the people gathered in the courtyard, and above all seeing the little boys with their heads shaved looking like egg shells, each attended by an auntie. Though the ceremony is symbolically supposed to make one an adult, it didn't really make any difference to the way I felt about my little brother, but it did serve to remind me that we were all growing up, and I was still behind.

Class 7 was a much better year academically, proving the wisdom of giving up on the skipping, with English Composition up to 52.3 and maths a startling 70%. Remarks were more the effect of "Keep it up", and "Good". I was beginning to find myself and could see that mathematics was going to be my strong point.

On the other hand, up to this time, I could not have had much of a social life, though I did start visiting Chitwan with my sisters during the 2-month winter holiday. We had a maternal uncle there with whom we could stay, and there were twelve other cousins around to play with. It gave me a chance to see a very different part of the country, the low-lying plains known as the Tarai, where it is very hot in the summer, but perfect in the winter. In the park I could even be a tourist and see the wild animals. This was not as spectacular as it might have been, since one year Crown Prince Dipendra was on a hunting trip and much of the park was closed, and the winter season was the time when the grass was cut back and the tigers never showed themselves. All I remember seeing were rhinoceros and deer, though I did get to ride an elephant. Back in school, though, the children in my class were still smaller than me, and while I experienced no real problems, it was not until Class 8 that I remember really joining in social activities. At this time I was 16 and was only 2 years older than my classmates.

It was also when I was 16 that I had one of my worst experiences ever with a journalist, this time from *India Today*. I didn't particularly want to talk with him, and neither did my family, but he said he only wanted to take some photographs and wouldn't take up much of our time. We let him take some in the house, but he came back to complain that the light had not been good enough, and suggested a trip to Bhaktapur, a beautiful and largely restored historical city towards the eastern end of the valley. I didn't want to go, but he was so pushy that eventually we agreed.

It was not as if I was a professional model, and on the way we told him that I did not want to be the centre of a public spectacle. He agreed, saying that he would use a zoom lens so that no one would even see that I was being photographed. It is less than an hour to Bhaktapur, but by the time we got there, I was car-sick from the bumpy road and the exhaust fumes from trucks, tractors and buses. The photographer, completely disregarding my objections, began snapping me every step I took, and soon a curious crowd gathered. I was beginning to lose my temper when he apparently got what he wanted: a photo of me looking particularly angry.

No one ever bothered to send us any of the photos, or the write up. We only saw the piece later translated into Nepali. What was written was that anyone could see from my photo that I spent my life being angry and upset, that I seldom smiled, and that I disliked being with my family. It was the first of several bad experiences with the Indian media. In another case a film maker kept pressuring me to give away the secret traditions associated with Kumari. Most of these I did not even know since I had been a child at the time and they were never explained to me. But though I did know a few secrets, I had never divulged anything even to my sisters, and I never will. He was very pushy and thoroughly obnoxious, and was mainly interested in making a documentary on the day Kumari changes. I'm happy to say that he was never able to make his film. In general we have found that representatives of the Indian media treat us with a kind of colonial mentality and twist facts so much that we are no longer even willing to talk with them.

In Class 8 I started wearing glasses. My family all said it was because of eating too much tomato *achar*. We believe that tomatoes can be bad for the eyes, and even our doctor warned me to cut back. It may have also had something to do with the way I had been allowed to sit right in front of the TV screen when I had been Kumari. Of course no one was allowed to sit between me and the screen, and I continued the same habit for a while when I came home. I'm not sure what would happen if a Kumari had failing eyesight when in office and had to wear glasses. Would this be considered a disqualifying blemish, or would she just get little red glasses?

Despite the glasses, by Class 8 I was beginning to interact better with my classmates, and beginning to feel far more a part of our group. In particular there was a picnic that my scout group went on to Sundarijal at the northern end of the valley. This is a lovely picnic spot high up in a water-shed and to get there we had to climb for about 45 minutes with clear water cascading on either side of us. As scouts we had a special scarf, but no uniform, and the different groups had a kind of competition among themselves to cook the meal. My sister, Samjhana, was on the same picnic, though we would not actually be classmates until the next year. Her group was to cook the *tarkari* (vegetable curry) while mine was to do the rice. Perhaps it is an indication of how going to school has changed traditional life that some of us, and not only the girl who had spent 8 years sequestered in her temple, found these simple tasks difficult. We first collected wood for the fires, but while Samjhana's *tarkari* turned out fine, one of the girls in my group had the idea that once the water in the rice started to boil, you should pour it out. As a result, we made rice that was half-cooked: soft on the outside, but hard on the inside. It didn't matter. Everyone was so hungry that they ate it all up. I'm surprised there were no stomach aches.

It was while I was in Class 8 that a Japanese film crew began coming during Indra Jatra and asked if they could film me. Their plan was to come every year and to see what changes I had gone through during the year. There were actually two crews, one from TBS and the other from NHK, but I tend to get them confused, and they seem to have traded some of their footage around for their final results.

The Japanese were enjoyable to work with. They were sincerely interested in what they were doing, and I find that there is a kind of bond between us and the Japanese. They were always respectful (of our culture, I mean, not of me) and seemed to understand us easily. There must be more similarities between our cultures than between ours and those of the West. When we were filming, the Japanese crew seemed to be able to read my facial expressions, and to tell when something they had asked me to do made me uneasy or uncomfortable. Actually, while I particularly liked working with the Japanese, my experiences with film-makers generally have been positive, while with print journalists and photographers I never know whether to trust them or not.

At first, however, I had been reluctant to work with film makers because one of the worst misrepresentations of Kumari had been the first Nepali-made colour feature film, entitled "Kumari". It had been made a long time before, possibly even before I had moved into Kumari Che, but we only saw it when it was broadcast on Nepal Television in about 1992. It was really appalling: poorly researched (if researched at all), completely made up and having no basis in reality. The plot centred around an ex-Kumari living in a fancy apartment who was in love. She and the guy were planning to get married, but she had a dream in which she saw that by marrying him she would cause his death. And of course, she had also been chosen after being in a dark room full of buffalo heads. Before this film came out I don't think many people in Nepal knew or cared about the Kumari curse legend, and not only did the film tell a story without any basis in reality, but it did a great deal of harm as Nepali tour guides and interpreters became convinced of the truth of the legend.

Documentary makers, however, worked in a completely different way, and came out with completely different results. It was fun sometimes living out scenes from my life, like when we filmed at my school, and I went into a class of five-year-olds. It was quite funny, because when it had actually happened, I was twelve, whereas when we filmed I was about 16. Another scene I particularly remember was of shopping and cooking with my mother. Our relations had improved dramatically since that first year or two, and even on the screen we look quite comfortable with one another as we go out shopping for fish, which we bring home, then clean, cut up and cook.

The crew had an interesting problem filming that scene. While in my grandparents' time foreigners and others not of our caste wouldn't even have been allowed inside the house, today caste restrictions in our society are largely breaking down. At school and college, we generally make friends with people without regarding their caste, and we certainly never ask a person's caste before admitting them to the house. However, the Shakyas do retain a ban on strangers, and some other Newari castes, entering their kitchens where the family shrine is located. Undaunted, the Japanese crew set up a kind of studio in the front room, and somehow we got the fish cooked.[1]

Filming could be enjoyable as long as it was inside the house. I never had to do any actual acting, I just had to behave normally.

---

[1] I didn't actually see the final result for years until some friends took me to a Japanese restaurant in Thamel for lunch. The waiters there recognised me and said they had a documentary about me if I would like to watch it. I was a little surprised to see that the Japanese had made some of the usual mistakes, including the rather fantastic claim that Kumari's identity is kept completely secret, that no one knows who her family is or where she comes from. This would obviously be impossible in a society as small as ours.

Outside, however, I found it quite embarrassing doing retakes over and over again. A crowd would always gather and people would begin speculating about what was going on. When I had been Kumari the crowds had always known exactly what was going on at festivals and who I was, while I had known exactly what was expected of me. This was very different, and I often found myself rather more conspicuous than I liked to be.

The original Japanese plan was to keep filming every year and to follow how I was getting along. Unfortunately, we received so much criticism and pressure from certain conservative sectors of the Shakya community, who felt that the life of an ex-Kumari should not be displayed, that we had to withdrew from the project after about three years.

My studies were now quite challenging, and it was during this year that I achieved my ambition of "lighting the lamp" and staying up late at night studying by the light of the small table lamp the way Pramila had been doing when I first came home. I got through English 1 (comprehension) with 49%. Yet I managed to fail both English 2 with 34.5% and my old friend English composition, though at 39.3% I came close. Science was disappointing as well at 49%. On the other hand I was doing extremely well in maths: 76.3%, and was also taking optional maths in which I got 71.8%. The teacher's remarks told me that I had to work hard during vacation.

In the vacation between Classes 8 and 9 we were approached by a German film maker named Ursala Bayer. As with the Japanese, I found her very easy to work with. She was doing a documentary about not only the royal Kumari, but the Kumaris of Bhaktapur, Patan and Bungamati as well. I only had a small part concerning what an ex-Kumari does in her school holidays, and we filmed in Nagarkot on the edge of the Valley, and in Chitwan. I didn't have to be interviewed, and there were only a few shots of me roaming around. It was fun to do and we were pleased with the results.

From Goddess to Mortal

Classes 9 & 10 are the years we use to prepare for the SLC Exam which is based on the work we do in those two years. I was joined in those grades by Samjhana,[1] and though my sisters remained my closest friends, I was joining in more and more with the other kids in group activities. During this year the boys and the girls seemed to grow closer together. Up to that time we had always done everything separately. I don't mean by this that relationships in the Western sense were starting. We are still a very conservative society. It is just that our shyness with one another seemed to evaporate, and from that time on we always played together in tiffin breaks. We became like a big family. I suppose we were a little immature, since our favourite game was "hide and seek", but it was fun, and a good way to relieve the stress of studying for the most important examination of our young lives.

During Class 9 was when the most successful and well-known of the documentaries I was associated with was filmed. This was a Danish production for children's TV called simply "Kumari". It was filmed in an interesting way, using the Bungamati Kumari and the Bungamati Kumari Ghar. Bungamati is a very traditional and very religiously important Newari village south of Patan. One of the principal deities of the valley, called Rato Machendranath, spends half of the year in Patan and half in Bungamati, and there is a Kumari there even though it was never a royal capital.

A lot of people writing about the Royal Kumari have used either the Patan Kumari or the Bungamati Kumari as their model since these two Living Goddesses are less secretive than the Royal Kumari. They live in their own homes with their

---

[1] It might be remembered that Samjhana had also been a Kumari candidate at the same time I was. She has always said that she was never sorry not to have been chosen, but that she is proud to have a sister who was Kumari.

families, and except for one or two big festivals their ceremonial duties are fairly minimal. But since the rules governing the lives of the different Kumaris vary, this may have led to some of the mistakes when writing about the Royal Kumari. For example, as I understand it, the Bungamati Kumari has much stricter rules about cuts and scratches and losing a tooth: as a result, they are seldom in office for more than two or three years, and may even lose their divinity if there is no immediate replacement.[1]

I had no idea what was going on or what the script was like as the filming progressed, and in fact I think that it changed as they went along. At first they weren't even sure if they were going to use the parts about me or not. The end result was interesting. Except that they put in the bit about being kept in a dark room with buffalo heads (I did not know about this during filming), the story was generally true in spirit, although a lot of the details were in fact made up. Perhaps it tended to play on the emotions a little too much, since it gave the impression that it was forbidden for a Kumari to have any pets or touch any animals. Kumari's forbidden relationship with a small dog played a prominent part. In fact, the only animal I would not be allowed to touch, in common with all Shakyas, would be a pig. Again, I was not called upon to act or speak, but kind of hung out in the background sort of remembering episodes of my life as they were played out by the Bungamati Kumari.

Perhaps I was enjoying myself too much with my friends and spending too much time filming, since in Class 9 I got some of the worst marks of my scholastic career. I failed both English courses with 31 and 37% in English 1 and 2, and even failed Science with 37%. The work was, in fact, becoming far more difficult. "Science" comprised physics, chemistry and biology, and all questions were based on SLC questions, which were bound to be tough.

---

[1] They are also of Bajracharya rather than Shakya caste.

"Why don't you try reading English magazines?" Pramila asked me, trying to be helpful.

"I don't want to. Why should I?" I still had bad memories of Pramila's *Newsweek*.

"You have to do something about your English. Maybe if you could find some magazines that interest you, you might improve. If you fail Class 9, you won't be able to go on to Class 10, and then you won't be able to take the SLC."

"I'll be okay. My mathematics marks will get me through. Why can't I just concentrate on what I'm good at?"

In fact my mathematics mark was a spectacular 87%. But you can't only do one subject, and the teachers' remarks seemed designed to give me a good kick where it would hurt. "Needs guidance at home ... Very intelligent but shaky (Don't you just hate it when you are told you are not working up to your potential?) ... Needs special care .... Unsatisfactory." One thing we decided was that I didn't need any distractions in Class 10, so that if anyone approached us about doing a film, we would politely decline.

I remember that year's trip to Chitwan for a particular event. One day when our uncle took us walking in the jungle, we got tired and stopped at a house for a rest. The house was the type we don't have in the hills, up on stilts with no ground floor. Inside the house was a poster of me as Kumari. I wouldn't have said anything, but Surmila was with us and asked the woman there if she knew who the girl in the picture was.

"All I know is that she is a special goddess for the health and prosperity of children, and she is called Kumari. Even the king worships her. I do puja to her picture every day."

"What would you do if you had the girl in the picture right in front of you?" Surmila asked.

"What do you mean? She is a goddess and she lives in Kathmandu."

"But she changes about every eight years. There is a different girl now. The girl in that picture is my sister here."

The woman took a good look at me, and shook her head to show that she didn't believe it.

"Look again, then look at the picture." She did look again, but remained unconvinced. Admittedly, the photo was of me at my most intense taken in full regalia at Indra Jatra during my last year, a photo that is still widely displayed. In the end I was relieved that she didn't recognise me, since I don't know what she might have done.

Class 10 I remember as being another year of social events, especially picnics with my classmates. In mid-winter, we all went to Pulchowki, which, though it is on the south-eastern edge of the valley, at 2765 metres is the highest of the surrounding hills, and the only one except for Nagarkot that ever gets any snow. In January, the valley always gets a couple of weeks of rain, and this will fall as snow on Pulchowki peak, making it the most accessible place for valley people to get into the snow. In common with most of my classmates, I had never been in snow before, and was excitedly looking forward to the experience.

We arrived about 9 in the morning, got off the bus and started climbing. Every one was 15 or 16 except for me. I was 18, but no longer noticed the age difference, and was as carefree as they were. I certainly felt no more mature than them, or in any way a leader. About 11 we stopped for our packed lunch, at the half-way point. Unfortunately, it had not rained the night before, so the snow had melted back and we had to go right to the top to find any. It was great when we reached the snow: everyone started throwing it at one another and we were all slipping and sliding all over the place, though I did well to keep my footing. Then we ate the rest of our food around 3, spent another hour playing around, then started back down about 4.

The Newars are city people, and not natural mountaineers like the Sherpas or other mountain dwellers from the north of

Nepal. It had never occurred to us that if it had taken us from 9-3, 6 hours, to go up, that it would take at least half that amount of time to get back down. We were just having so much fun that we forgot all about it, and we enjoyed slipping and sliding back down.

"I think we'd better get a move on," suggested someone.

"Why should we when we are having so much fun?"

"Because it is getting dark." We all stopped playing around for a moment, and noticed that what she had said was true. Even though we had gone for the snow, we had forgotten that it was mid-winter.

"It will be pitch dark by six," said one of the boys. "I wonder how much further it is?" In fact, it was still a very long way, and once it got difficult to see, we had to slow down.

"I hope the bus driver waits for us," moaned one of the girls.

Someone fell down, and we heard her scream. "What is it?"

"My wrist! I think I broke it."

It was a moonless night, and we could not even see the person in front of us. Eventually we made it down about 7:30 or 8 only to see the bus starting to pull away.

"Wait! Don't leave us!" we screamed. Luckily he heard us and stopped.

"Where were you going?"

"You only paid me for a day trip."

By the time we got back worried parents were phoning the school.

But the biggest event of this year for me was something I would never even have dreamed of: a trip to New York. The Danish film had won the prize of Best Documentary at the HBO Children's Film Festival, and I was invited to attend, all expenses paid, as a special guest. Though we had decided I would not do any filming during this year, my family felt that this would be a once in a life-time opportunity, and so enthusiastically agreed. I suddenly remembered the two little foreign girls who used to come and play with me at the bottom of the steps in Kumari Che.

"Will I be able to meet Maya and Laxmi there?" I asked. In spite of all my schooling, my ideas of the world at large were still rather vague.

"Do you even know what country they are from?" asked Pramila, being irritatingly practical.

"Well, no ..."

"You could just ask around on the streets. Maybe somebody there will have seen them somewhere in the world." I felt silly.

I'm sure I must be the first former Kumari ever to travel abroad, and certainly to the United States. And so protected had my life been up to now, that I had never even been to Kathmandu's Tribhuvan International Airport. It was very strange when we got there, because as I stood outside the airport with my family, a whole bus load of Japanese people started waving at me. At first, I wasn't sure if it was me they were waving at, and looked over my shoulder.

"Who are they waving at," I asked Pramila.

"You, I think."

"Why?"

"I don't know. Why don't you try waving back and see what happens?"

So I did, and as soon as I waved back, they all piled off the bus and came over to speak to me. It turned out that they had seen one of the Japanese TV documentaries, and were all interested in talking to me and having their photo taken with me. Here I was going off as a guest to a film festival in New York, and I felt like an celebrity before I had even gone into the airport.

Inside the airport, everything was new to me from checking in my luggage to going through passport control. And of course I had never seen anything like the inside of the plane. It was a little reminiscent of a bus, but much cleaner and more comfortable. I was hoping that my stomach would behave.

The flight took a round about route, going first to Singapore, then to Frankfurt, then finally to New York. As anyone would be on a first flight, I was a little nervous, and wished I could have had my old Kumari equanimity back. Whether there was any more turbulence than usual, I am not sure, but the flight seemed very bumpy to me. Fortunately it was a different movement from that of a bus, and I didn't need to use the airsick bag. I had plenty of company besides, since the Japanese were on the same flight and kept stopping by to chat to me, get my address and take more photos. Their English was about as rudimentary as mine, so we understood one another on a basic level. At least I was communicating.

The Nepali cameraman from the film was with me to guide me through the intricacies of changing planes in Singapore. After Singapore I felt like an old hand at flying, and wasn't nervous for the second leg. Though I was suspicious of the food (I'm a bit suspicious of anything not cooked at home or by a relative), I had asked for vegetarian meals, and managed to eat something. At Frankfurt airport it was snowing outside, and I spent most of the two-hour layover staring at the falling snow, remembering Pulchowki, and wishing I could play in it.

By the time we got to New York I was so tired out from the long flight that I did not get much of a first impression on the long ride into town. Once I had reached my 33rd floor room (which did not have a key, but opened with a card, something that fascinated me the entire week) and phoned home, I just went straight to sleep.

If this, my first trip abroad, is anything to judge by, I am not a natural traveller. The excitement of being in a new place was over-powered by how much I missed my family as well as worry over an upcoming exam. I was only there for a week, and I don't think I ever quite got over the culture shock. I had taken the precaution of packing my suitcase full of food: instant noodles, cashew nuts, even chocolate. It wasn't that I thought chocolate didn't exist in the United States, but I didn't know if I would have the courage to buy it. Whether it was excitement or jet lag, or just the novelty of the situation, I had very little appetite the whole time I was there, and don't remember eating anything at the hotel except chips, mashed potatoes, and a bit of chow mein. The latter at least was familiar from Kathmandu where it has been popularised by Tibetan refugees. The only thing I remember enjoying was ice cream. That I did not get ill from my poor diet was probably only because of the members of the close-knit Nepali community—some of them were working in Nepali films, others were musicians and some worked in restaurants—who invited me for meals in the big flat they all shared. Of course they asked me the same old questions, but at least I got a good meal in return.

I was taken for an interview at CNN that turned out to be a complete disaster. First of all, I had to wait a long time, though no one explained why. Then I had to go through having all the facial make-up put on. No one prepared me for the sort of things that would be asked, so when I went into the studio I had no idea what to expect. In all my previous interviews, there had always been a real person in front of me. This time as I stood alone in the studio, I heard a disembodied voice which seemed to come at once from nowhere and everywhere, and was in English besides. I completely freaked out and was unable to say a word. At least we got a couple of nice pictures out of it.

Much better, and one of my best memories, was when I was interviewed by a group of children ranging from about 5-8 who had seen the film. I could understand their questions, but was not confident enough of my English to answer, so answered through Nepali students who interpreted. Their questions were very different from what I was asked by friends in Nepal. Not one of them asked me about getting married since that was not part of the film (and that is undoubtedly one of the reasons I enjoyed the interview so much). One of the things they wanted to know was if the *ghazal* I wore around my eyes ever hurt or got into my eyes. But what they were most interested in was the name of the little dog, and they laughed their heads off when I told them it was "Tiger".

My days were so busy, what with attending the film festival, being interviewed (disastrously and otherwise), trying to figure out the lifts in the hotel (for some reason Reception seemed to be in the middle rather than on the ground floor), being taken on a tour of the sights, and eating with the Nepali community, that I never had any trouble sleeping. Though I missed my family, the solitary splendour of my hotel room was a little reminiscent of my eight years as Kumari when I had always slept in a room by myself, though the street here was a lot further away.

7

Exciting and different as the trip to New York had been, the exam I would have to take on my return was in the back of my mind the whole time. This was something called the SLC Sent Up exam, and was a sort of barrier or pre-qualifying exam that anyone wanting to take the SLC had to pass. If I had failed it, I would not have been able to take the SLC, so it was difficult to get it out of my mind in spite of the distractions of the trip. Luckily, I did well enough, even though it began the day after I returned. I don't think I ever really got over my jet-lag in New York, because when I came back I had no problem.

After going all the way to New York and back on an airplane, a school trip to Changu Narayan, the oldest temple in the valley on a hill north of Bhaktapur, might be seen as a bit of a let-down. But I was so happy to be back, and so relieved that my exam was over, that I thoroughly enjoyed it. This time we went out for the day and cooked our own food at the foot of the hill. I'm glad to say we got the rice right this time. Though I climbed the hill to the temple with my friends, I was just concentrating on having a good time, and it never occurred to me that I was now visiting a god who used to come and visit me twice every year.

Back at the foot of the hill was a small river, and the only crossing was a single plank. Being afraid of this, I took my shoes off and started wading across. Another of my friends followed me, and being kids, we started splashing one another. When our friends saw us, they all came running down to the river, and soon we were engaged in a general splashing match. It felt great while we were doing it, but soon after that we had to get in the bus and go back home. It wasn't long till we were all shivering. I still hated public buses, but being with a crowd of friends was different, and I didn't even mind being wet and shivering.

All these experiences brought us closer together, and back in school we had moved on from hide and seek to an even sillier game called "Crocodile Ocean" which all 40 of us now played together. We all formed a circle, hand-in-hand, sang the "Crocodile Ocean" song, counted to ten, and if you were the tenth person, you tried to slap the hand of the person behind you. If you succeeded, they were out, if you missed, you were out. We played this game with an odd intensity, as if we knew that we would soon go through another of our life-cycle rituals and be separated. Something of our enthusiasm communicated itself to the younger students, and the whole school used to come out to watch how older and more mature students behaved.

With the exception of the trip to New York, the things I have been relating are only the kind of experiences that any Kathmandu teenager in Grade 10 might have. It is precisely because there is nothing unusual about them that I have gone to the trouble of telling them. I was no longer the girl who was so out of place that she had to sit and look out the windows at the other kids playing at recess time. I had become almost boringly normal, and my life as Kumari was relegated to the past where it belonged.

Another step forward in Class 10 was when I took up dancing. For Parent's Day, which was also the 25th anniversary of the school, all the Class 10 students had to perform, and I decided to participate in the dance program. I had always loved dancing, and in Kumari Che had sometimes made my playmates be an audience for me, or if there was no one around had danced in front of the reflective glass in front of the full-sized portrait of King Mahendra. Now was my chance to see if I could really do it.

It was not as if I was the only one on the stage. There were ten of us, five boys and five girls, and it was a Newari dance called

"Gha juya jaka Khoiegy kha ji" ("Because There is Pain in my Heart"). This dance, and particularly the song that went with it, were often used in protests demanding full political rights for the Newari language, and before we were allowed to perform it, Pramila had to translate the words into Nepali for the Vice-Principal in case it proved too controversial.

I was very excited, but not really nervous about it, and thoroughly enjoyed the performance. Judging from the reaction of the audience, they had enjoyed it too, and not all of them realised they were watching the same girl they might have seen pulled around on a chariot at Indra Jatra 6 or 7 years before. For me, it was one more step in coming out of my shell. Nowadays my sisters tell me that I no longer walk, but dance up and down the stairs and along the street. Strange to remember that when I first came home I didn't even know how to walk properly and used to clomp. The dance itself proved such a success that it was always included in the programs of later years.

But the point of Class 10 was not picnics, games, dancing or trips to New York. The point was to get ready for the long-anticipated SLC exam. So while we played when we could, we also studied very hard. Our marks on exams and class work were irrelevant. The only thing that mattered was what we did on the exam. The object was to get the all-important First Division (60%+), which would give us the option of studying whatever subject we wanted in the future.

At this point I had no idea what I wanted to do with the rest of my life. I only knew that I had to do as well as I possibly could in the exam, so I approached it strategically. English was more or less hopeless. I would do what I could, but could expect nothing spectacular. Nepali had always been one of my stronger subjects, but Nepali is notoriously difficult to get a good mark in at SLC level. Therefore I would have to play to my strengths and go for maximum points in maths in hopes that the two maths papers would pull up my over-all average.

Just like Pramila had been doing when I first came home, during the winter vacation, just seven years after I had first entered coaching class, I did extra classes. But I concentrated on mathematics, not wanting to be distracted.

The exam was really gruelling. There were seven separate papers of three hours each from 7 to 10 every morning. With Saturday off, that meant it was held over 8 days. There were a number of different exam centres, and the one chosen for me was only about ten minutes walk away.

It was only on the first day, what with going to a new school and starting on the eight-day ordeal with the particularly difficult Nepali exam, that I was a little nervous. As on any school day, I did a brief puja to Ganesh and Saraswati, but did no extra pujas. If I was not ready now, the gods would not help me. Once I got through that first day and had managed the huge amount of writing for the Nepali exam, the others did not frighten me. Even for English, I was confident that I could do what I needed to. But even so, for all of my subjects except Mathematics, I stayed up until midnight or even 1 AM studying. The two nights before the maths papers, I was so confident that I was in bed by eight, feeling that being well-rested was more important than anything new I could learn.

Possibly the worst part of the SLC is waiting for the results, for it takes two months before they are ready. When the big day that we had been waiting for came, we knew that the results would be published in the national government newspaper, the *Ghorkhapatra*. In it, if we had passed, we would find our number and the division in which we had passed. Detailed results would later be delivered to our schools, but for the moment, knowing the division would be enough.

The results were due to be out at 6 am, and at that time, Samjhana and I were at the *Ghorkhapatra* stand on Dharma Path near the end of New Road, since the papers on this particular day would not get anywhere near our local shops. The street was crowded with students, all desperate to get their results, and it was raining besides. Then the papers were late, and we had to stand for three hours in the rain until they finally arrived. When they did come, there was a near mob scene as everyone fought to get a copy.

With Samjhana, I joined the unruly crowd grabbing at pages until I finally got hold the page with my number on it, but in the wet and the scramble, my result had been torn off. I fought my way back to where I could get hold of another copy, and could hardly believe it when I saw the result: the coveted First Division I had studied so hard for.

I was not, by the way, the first former Kumari to have taken and passed the SLC. Nani Maya Shakya, who was Kumari during the late 60s and early 70s had completed her SLC and opened a pharmacy. Another, Harsha Laxmi Shakya, who had been Kumari between 1955 and 1961, had even become a nurse, though we have two ways of entering nursing, either from 8th grade or 10th, and I am not sure which path she took.

When I learned the details of my marks, I found that I had got comfortably into the first division with an overall average of 70.25%. Even in English I got 64%. Nepali was by far the lowest at 48%, but that was no worse than average for the year. In compulsory maths I managed 82%, but in Optional Maths and Statistics I came through with a whopping 90%. My strategy of concentrating on maths to pull my average up seemed to have paid off.

The future, it seemed, was mine. What was I going to do with it?

* * * *

The first thing I needed was something to fill my time in the few months between the SLC exam and the beginning of my Intermediate Science Certificate course. Learning to knit was all very well, but I had become so accustomed to being busy that I needed something to more than just a hobby. Again, I followed in Pramila's footsteps when the headmistress of my old school asked me if I would like to teach part-time while I waited for the course to begin. So I agreed to teach grades 5 & 6, Health Science and Moral Science. I suppose it is logical enough to have an ex-goddess teaching Moral Science.

Since I am naturally a little shy, I might have been expected to have been nervous about teaching, but since not only Pramila, but Surmila as well had gone through the same experience, it seemed just another right of passage like *ihi* or *bahrah*. Perhaps I was also so accustomed to being with children younger than me, that standing in front of the class seemed no different from being part of it. And it was a lot easier than standing in front of lights and TV cameras in the CNN studio. Though the textbooks were all in English, explanations in class were given in Nepali to make sure everyone understood.

I don't know if any of my students realised that their Moral Science teacher, standing there telling them to respect their elders and help out in emergencies, was a former Kumari. No one ever asked, and there was no reason for me to volunteer the information. I also tutored the occasional weak student in mathematics at home. For a few months anyway, I was making between 1400 and 1800 rupees a month, and I was proud to give some to my father to help pay for my keep.

The choice of what college to attend for ISC was not difficult. The essential choice was between a private or a government run college, and this was taken entirely out of my hands. Private colleges were simply too expensive. My "pension" had been raised by the government to 1000 rupees a month, and while this is not an entirely insignificant amount for a young, unqualified girl in an economy like Nepal's, it continued to go into the family kitty. The most expensive years for any family are when there are teenage children around, and though my parents had managed private schools for us up to SLC, after that we were on our own. Both my older sisters, Pramila and Surmila, had studied at Amrit Science College, just north of Thamel and more or less next to the Malla Hotel. They warned me that the atmosphere was very different from what I had become used to, but it did have the reputation of producing the best science results in the country.

Students who achieve a First Division in SLC can go on to study whatever subjects they want, but no one who gets below First Division is allowed to take up maths and sciences. During my time in classes 9 and 10, I had started sketching houses, and wondering how they were built. Gradually the idea grew on me that I would like to design houses myself, and my sisters told me that field I should go in for was architectural engineering. Once I get an idea into my head, as you might have noticed by this point, I am fairly hard-headed, and it is hard to budge me. Though my sisters had also warned me that architecture is one of the most difficult subjects to get into, that made little impression. To gain admittance to a government university or to get a scholarship to a private one, marks of around 80-90% are required in a wide variety of subjects. 60-70% would be enough for entrance to a private university, though without a scholarship this would be impossible for me. But I wasn't worried. I had succeeded so far, and I was convinced I would succeed now.

Before I went to the college for the first time, Pramila took me aside for a chat. "It's time you started acting your age," she told me.

"What do you mean?"

"You've been asking us for help ever since you started school. But you're a big girl now. You've passed your SLC and you're going to be a college student. It's time you started to figure things out for yourself."

I know that she did not mean me any harm. Quite the contrary, she simply wanted me to be more self-reliant and less dependent on others, but still, it worried me and made me wonder if I would be able to handle the task ahead of me. I began the two-year course with less confidence than I would have liked.

A more immediately helpful suggestion at this point was that I not even bother to turn up at Amrit Science College for the first few days. My sisters had learned that the classes never started when they should, so I waited until the semester was about a week old.

On my first day, as would be the case for the next two years, in order to arrive at college by 6:30, I had to leave the house at 6 am when it was only just light, and though the coldest days of winter had passed, there was still a chill in the air. My walk took me through Durbar Square, just by my old home in Kumari Che, then through Indra Chowk and past Seto Machendranath to Ason Tole. All of these places held, or should have held, memories for me, since I had been either pulled by them in my chariot or carried by them on my palanquin. Yet I was cold, and alone: Samjhana, who had elected to study arts rather than sciences, had gone to a different college. The future was again more important to me than the past, and I did not stop to dwell on when I had been the centre of attention.

Continuing from Ason, I walked through Jhata and part of Thamel, more of a foreign settlement than part of Kathmandu, with its guest houses and restaurants, and full of the foreigners who used to come and see me at my temple. Yet at this time of the morning, it was too early for them to be up or for any of the trekking and souvenir shops which catered for them to be open. When I passed Baghwan Baha, which had been one of my most important and liveliest stops during Bahi Dyah Jatra, I didn't even recognise where I was.

The first look at Amrit Science College was not reassuring. The school where I had spent the past 7 years studying and teaching, had been a pleasant place, painted a cheerful white, and repainted often enough that it always looked new. These buildings, however, were of stark concrete which had never known a coat of paint. Nor did they look as if they were very often cleaned. They were imposing, and certainly not what you could call welcoming. Luckily, amidst all the milling crowd of students there were two friendly faces, my friends Mamta and Jasmine from school.

"Rashmila, over here!" they called to me, and I found them standing with several other girls. They introduced me as plain Rashmila, and the seven of us were to remain friends through the two years of college. I needed some girlfriends. The vast majority of the students were boys, and they were from all over the country. Some of the ones from the Tarai were very dark and looked more Indian than Nepali, while the ones from the northern hills were lighter skinned and oriental looking. Most of them spoke with strange accents, wore strange clothes and had rough manners. The boys all swaggered a bit and looked as if they were trying to prove themselves to one another now that they had left their villages and were in the capital.

"There is a Physics lecture at 6:30. Maybe we should go to that," suggested one of the girls. There didn't seem to be a regular course of study. You just went to the lectures that would be most helpful to you. In this case it was not very helpful at all. We were a little late and so had to sit on broken benches near the back. The lecture hall was huge, capable of holding over a hundred students. There had only been 40 students in my entire classes 9 and 10. We couldn't hear a thing. Not only were the acoustics terrible, but the lecturer droned on in a monotone that was soon lost amidst the conversations of all the boys who were not even putting up the pretence of listening. I came out having not even bothered to open my notebook to take notes.

"Didn't learn much from that," commented one of my new friends as we came out. "Maybe the next one will be better." It wasn't. It was meant to be a chemistry lecture, but in this case the lecturer didn't even bother to turn up. Being new, we waited, and at least it gave us a chance to get to know one another.

"Maybe it will be 3rd time lucky," I said hopefully as we headed to a scheduled lecture in mathematics, my favourite subject. This time we were surprised to find seats empty near the front. Hopefully we took them, opened our notebooks and took out our pencils before we noticed that the boys sitting in the back had done neither. Instead they were loudly chewing bubble gum, blowing big bubbles, popping them all over their faces and laughing. When the lecturer came in, he wasn't much older than we were, and we could hear a ripple of derision from the students behind us as the young man nervously took up his position. A paper aeroplane flew past his head.

The lecturer had hardly begun when his voice was drowned out by rhythmic drumming from behind us. Then the boys began to accompany their drumming with singing. The lecturer attempted to raise his voice, but it was in vain. A swarm of paper planes engulfed him, and in despair, he picked up his lecture notes and ran off to shouts of triumph and catcalls from the boys. When the echoing, bare lecture hall had quieted down and we were leaving, one of my new friends, a little bolder than the rest of us, turned to some of the boys and asked, "Why did you do that?"

"What's your problem, little sister?" he asked. "Do you think you are still in school?"

"What's that supposed to mean?"

"Hey, discipline is for school kids. We've passed our SLC, we're college students now, and we can do what we want. If these so-called lecturers can't handle it, they shouldn't be here!"

It had not been a very good morning, and we gave up on lectures for a scheduled physics practical. At first we were pleasantly surprised that the lab was a big, clean room, and seemed to be well equipped with scales, pulleys, levers, lenses, mirrors and measuring devices. There were also bits of equipment that we didn't recognise.

"What do you suppose this is?" asked Jasmine.

"I don't know. Do you think we can touch it?"

"Maybe it is dangerous."

"Let's ask the teacher."

We looked around, but the only other people in the room were a few students, some looking as confused as we were, and a smaller group that seemed to be earnestly conducting an experiment.

"Maybe there is a demonstrator," I said. But no, there was no one but students. Shyly we approached the purposeful-looking group who were lining up pins in front of a mirror.

"Um, how do you know what to do?" we asked. Luckily, they were friendly.

"We find out from other students. Then we do the experiment, and pass on what we have learned. Just watch us, then you can sign out the apparatus and do it yourselves. The important thing is the measure the angle of the reflected image of the pins in the mirror."

This first day was all too typical. But there were variations. The Student's Union was riven with political factions. Sometimes while they were jockeying for power they might lock us in the labs, or out of the classrooms. We might turn up in the morning and find everyone locked out of the entire college. Or the administration might decide to have a welcoming or farewell ceremony and all classes would be cancelled. The whole thing was chaotic, and when I think back to those days, I remember an atmosphere more like that of a fish market than of an institution of learning. Just how Amrit Science College managed to turn out the best science results in the country has remained a mystery to me.

One of the most memorable incidents was during sports week when my friends and I went to watch a basketball game. Apparently the two teams represented two different political factions, and in the middle of it, a brawl broke out. Guys were throwing things, kicking and punching. It was the most violent scene I had witnessed since sitting on my chariot and watching guys fight for the holy *chang* in front of Seto Bhairav. But that had been good-natured, and I had been completely safe. These guys were out to cause real damage to one another, and were altogether too close for comfort. In the end, what we called the "union brothers", leaders of the students' union, helped the girls to escape, jumping over a wall, going through someone's house, and out to the main road so we could go home. If even in my post-Kumari life I had been rather protected up to now, I was learning what real life was like for most Nepali students.

For in fact I had now travelled about as far from my former life as it was possible to go. It would be difficult to be more protected than I had been during my early years in Kumari Che. When I ceased to be a divinity it might have seemed to me at first that I was thrown out into a harsh world, but in fact with my family and the pleasant surroundings of my private school, I was still relatively cocooned. Worst of all, I now seemed to have no one to turn to. Samjhana was studying different subjects in a different college, Surmila was studying at Ranpur in the Tarai. It seemed that not only had Pramila cut me off from the family's constant help, but I was in a wild and woolly world where there were no rules whatsoever, and I had to either sink or swim.

And yet some learning did go on. We discovered it was best to avoid lectures given by young lecturers because they were always crowded and turbulent. The older, more experienced and serious lecturers tended to attract smaller numbers of more enthusiastic students. And at least we could always be sure that practical labs would take place, even if we had to figure out ourselves how to do the experiments. Much of the disruption was caused by outside students. When I began, there was no uniform at the college, so that anyone could just come in, and often did. It was for some reason Commerce students from other campuses who came to visit friends who caused the most disruption. During my second year the administration decided on a policy of requiring uniforms and identity cards, and after that things got a little better.

My old school friends knew, of course, about my unusual childhood, but did not think it worth mentioning to the new friends they introduced me to. They only found out later from the occasional articles that appeared about me in the Nepali press. Then, to my amazement, they would ask me the same questions that everyone always asked. Couldn't anyone think of anything new? It was like a well-rehearsed interview, and not much different from back in Class 2, except that no one called me Kumari Didi.

"You were Kumari? Really? Is it true ..." I brace myself for what's coming. "... that you can never ..." Oh no, here it comes. "... get married? That anyone who marries you will die?" Sometimes one of my older friends who knew how much I hated this question, would rush to my rescue. But they were not always around.

Then depending on my mood, my questioner would either get a stark, "No!" or I would patiently explain that there were 7 or 8 former Kumaris in the valley ranging from Hira Maya Shakya who was now in her eighties and who had been happily married for nearly seventy years,[1] down to me. Of them, only my immediate predecessor and I were unmarried. One ex-Kumari had five children, and several were grandmothers. And if I wasn't married, it was because I was too busy getting an education, just like they were, and I had other things on my mind. So there!

In the atmosphere of the college, only the most brilliant of students could be expected to produce the kind of marks I would need if I was going to study to be an architectural engineer. Most harmful to my ambitions was the fact that the college gave no regular examinations except for the finals. In the run-up to SLC

---

[1] She passed away at the end of July, 2004 at the age of 88, survived by her 92-year-old husband.

there had been constant practice with model questions and practice exams. Whatever the merits of a system based only on standard examinations, if you are in it, you need to do everything possible to prepare yourself to pass them. Here, I simply did not get the practice I needed. I also learned gradually just the kind of competition I was facing. I would be up against the double hurdle of the ISC exam, and then the actual university entrance exam. The entrance exam would count for 70% of whether I would get what I wanted or not. The other 30% was made up of equal parts ISC and SLC. There would be about 1500 students taking the entrance exam, and only 24 scholarships would be awarded.

It was probably inevitable that I would fail. But I was hard-headed, and refused to consider studying anything but architectural engineering. I just could not imagine what failure would be like. When I took the ISC final, the results were not encouraging. I only managed a Second Division with an overall average of 48%. Still, hoping for a miracle, I went for the entrance exam, where I found the questions were of a completely different type than those of the ISC, and that I was totally unprepared for them. It was like being in the CNN booth again, only this time the result was capable of changing the course of my life. I waited for the results with no hope. In fact I passed, but only just, and was nowhere near the top twenty-four.

And now for the first time in my life I had to deal with failure and disappointment. Retiring as Kumari was simply part of life. It had been hard to overcome, but there had been plenty of new things to keep me busy. Now all my dreams were shattered, and because of my own stubbornness, I had nothing to fall back on.

I also suddenly found myself with nothing to do. I was now 21 and since the age of 12 I had been struggling to catch up. Hard as it had been, I had always achieved each of my goals, through a combination of my own hard work and the encouragement and help of my sisters and parents, and then gone on to the next one. Now I could see nothing stretching ahead of me but emptiness.

Though my failure was at least partially my own fault, I began, for the first time, to feel bitter about my past. If I hadn't spent those years isolated in Kumari Che I wouldn't have fallen behind, and if I hadn't had to work so hard to catch up I would have been able to realise my full potential.

My sisters were more sensible. Realising that it was no good for me to sit around moping, they insisted that I take a computer course, since whatever happened to me, any educated person in today's world is lost without a good knowledge of computers. It was not what I wanted, but at least it gave me something to do. Pramila was also insistent that I should at least try to learn another foreign language. The Goethe Institute offered to give me free introductory German lessons, but I had no interest in Germany and felt no real affinity with German people, in spite of the positive experience I had had with the German documentary crew. Just about the only language that did interest me was Japanese, and I began private lessons, though they were interrupted before I was able to make much progress.

In the computer course, I had to start right at the beginning, learning to type and use basic programs like Word and Exel, and at first it all seemed rather pointless. At about this time, when I was at my lowest, I was angered by an article that appeared in the *Kathmandu Post*, one of our leading English-language dailies, which proved that foreigners do not have a monopoly when it comes to writing nonsense about Kumari. The misinformed description of the selection process was particularly lurid: "The experience ... together with the added effects of eerie and mournful sounds plus leaping demons in frightening masks is designed to terrify. Normal adults are afraid to go anywhere near this place." That was bad enough, but what really upset me was this bald statement near the end of the article. "In recent years, former Kumaris are provided for by the government. Special grants are given, and scholarships to prestigious institutions are provided."

This was too much. It was a local paper, and the author was Nepali, so he should have known better. With Pramila's help I wrote an angry letter which appeared under the heading, "Dazed and Confused": ".... I got stunned when I read the last paragraph .... This information puzzled me for a while because being a former Kumari, I have not obtained even a scholarship so far from a prestigious institution .... I am highly interested in doing BE in architecture. But because of my low percentage I was not able to compete with those students with a strong educational background. Nor am I able to join a private engineering college .... I would like to request all the writers not to write such things without knowing the facts first ...."

It is true that my pension had been raised again, this time to 3000 rupees (about $40) per month, and it had been extended for life rather then until my 22nd birthday. Plenty of people in Nepal have to work hard for much less. But to me that wasn't the point The pension was money for someone who it was assumed would never be capable of earning her own living. I didn't want a handout, I wanted to be able to stand on my own two feet. The pension was enough to feed and cloth me, but not enough to enable me to study what I wanted. I felt that if I had earned anything by my years in Kumari Che it was the right to a skill with which I would be able to support myself. It also seemed to me that a scholarship rather than a pension for life would have been not only more useful to me, but cheaper for His Majesty's government in the long run.

I did, in fact have the mysterious offer of a scholarship in the United States at this point. I cannot remember the details, like the name of the college, but I do remember that it did not offer what I was interested in studying. It did not seem worthwhile to try to struggle to get my English to the point where I could function as an American student if I was not going to be able to study a subject I was interested in. In addition, the scholarship was only for the tuition, so that I would have had to work for my living expenses. My family felt that with my English problems and my lack of experience, I would be overwhelmed by trying to support myself in a foreign environment, so I had to turn down this offer.

Perhaps we were getting better now at impressing our views on journalists, for an article that appeared at this time in *Marie Claire* is one of the few in which I have found nothing to complain about. Or maybe the people who write for *Marie Claire* are just better at listening, for in 2004 there was another good article in the same publication. Neither of these articles went on about bloody buffalo heads, and even the marriage comments were kept to a minimum. The only problem I found was that the editors seemed to give the authors such tight word limits that they could not help being a little superficial. But I was quite surprised when the article was reprinted in the normally reliable weekly, *The Nepali Times*, to find an old photo of me as Kumari with the caption, "On the last day of Indra Jatra, 1994, previous Kumari Rashmila Shakya appears with a co-Kumari." By 1994 I was in Class 4, and there is no such thing as a co-Kumari. I am flanked in the photo by Ganesh and Bhairav.

At first I found the computer course boring and I wondered why I was doing it, but when we began to get into programming languages, a new world began to open up for me. I began to see that I had limited myself too much by my refusal to compromise over architectural engineering, and that there might be a future for me in Information Technology. I was even more encouraged when I learned that for a Bachelor of Information Technology, I would only have to study English for one semester. Maybe there was more to life than architectural engineering after all.

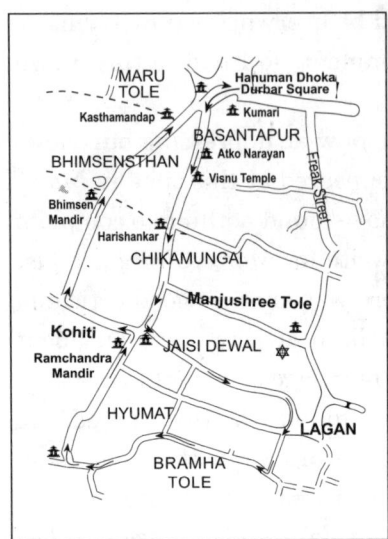

1st day of Indra Jatra *Konay Ya*

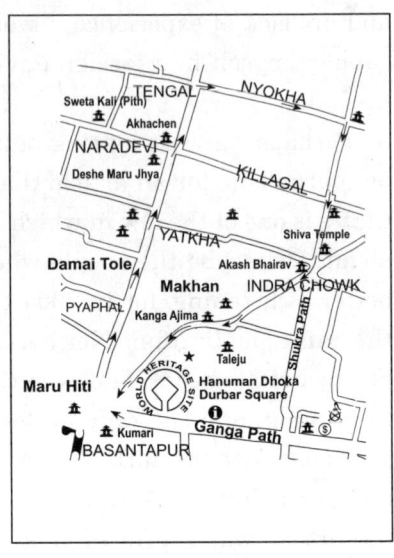

2nd day of Indra Jatra *Thanay Ya*

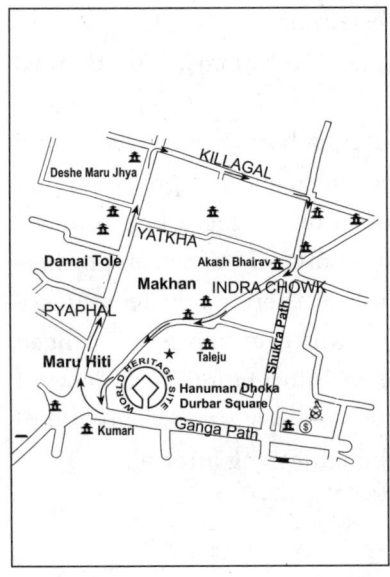

3rd day of Indra Jatra *Nahicha Ya*

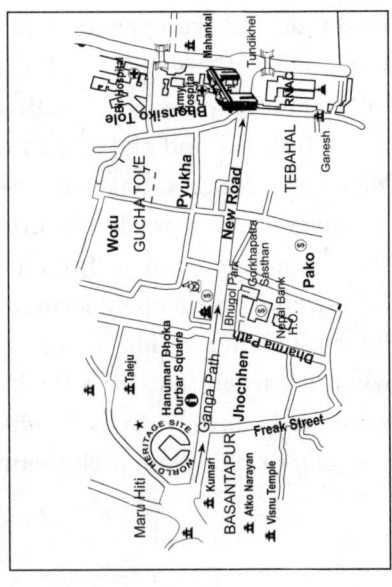

Ghode Jatra

8

In June, 2001, my successor as Kumari was replaced, and this was the occasion for a new spate of articles that seemed almost to go out of their way to misunderstand the nature of the Kumari tradition. It was particularly disappointing that respected international media outlets like the *Guardian* and the BBC would do such poor research. This time a new theme was "human rights", a theme to which I will return below.

All the old clichés were wheeled out yet again: the 108 buffalo and goat heads, the intimate physical examination and the marriage legend. I am not trying to claim that everything is perfect about the Kumari tradition. There *are* many aspects of it that can, and should, be criticized, but the criticism must come from an informed stance. A campaign to stop locking up a child in a room full of buffalo heads is likely to accomplish little when nothing like this happens in the first place.

The former Kumari, who was now plain Amita Shakya, was now faced with the same readjustment that I had previously faced. She was in theory better prepared, able to join a class of children her own age with teachers who were already familiar to her. To help her with her readjustment, her father asked me to go around and chat with her about the problems of adapting to her new life. Unfortunately, we did not really hit it off. Perhaps it was the age difference, or maybe just that we were very different people. Or she might have just felt she had to work out her life in her own way, and resented any interference. I certainly do not mean to imply any criticism of her, knowing how difficult those first few months can be. I doubt that I was much help to her, yet at least it is a step in the right direction to have previous Kumaris trying to help more recent ones with their adjustment. Perhaps we former Kumaris need to be more organised, or maybe we should even undergo some training in order to learn just how we can help the girls who come after us.

Eventually my own life took a big step for the better when I finally gave up my attachment to the idea of studying architectural engineering and decided to follow my new-found interest in computers. Pramila was now teaching in a college that offered a BIT (Bachelor in Information Technology) course, and perhaps feeling that her good intentions in forcing me more on my own devices had gone a little too far, she suggested that I apply. I was admitted, and took to the course even better than I expected (perhaps because I only had to do one semester of English) and have enjoyed making new friends as well. My marks are not spectacular, but are average or above, and if I graduate as expected in 2006, I will be the first (though I am sure not the last) former Kumari to obtain a bachelor's degree. I have kept up dancing as well, and enjoy being on stage at welcoming ceremonies for new students. And though I do not claim to be much good at it, I have even been part of a girls' basketball team in intramural competitions.

Throughout this narrative I have kept harping on certain themes, mostly concerning the mistakes that writers, both foreign and Nepali keep making again and again. I hope I have made it clear by this time that when I was 4 years old, I was not forced to spend a night in a room surrounded by 108 freshly severed goat and buffalo heads in order to prove my courage! Nor did I have to undergo a particularly rigorous physical examination. In fact, if you look at photographs of past Kumaris, it should be pretty obvious that we don't even look much like one another, so obviously we have not have to conform to any mythical physical ideal. If unusually fair skin had really been one of the criteria, I wouldn't have stood a chance.

I am not entirely sure of the origins of these misunderstandings, or if they possibly had a basis in reality in the past, and somewhere along the line became self-perpetuating. As early as 1880, H. Ambrose Oldfield—who had been the British Residency surgeon in Kathmandu for many years—in his *Sketches from Nepal*, told the Kumari story, complete with the little girl alone in the room full of severed heads and her difficulty in getting married. What his sources were he did not say. Were these things that were true at the time, or was he simply misinformed? I wonder if his story was simply accepted as fact and repeated over and over again. Getting at the truth has not been assisted by the traditional secrecy of the Newars about our traditions. It is this secrecy that has led scholars like Michael Allen, whose *Cult of Kumari* is the standard work on the subject, to look to the Patan or Bungamati Kumaris to fill in what they could not learn of the Royal Kumari. Allen is quite open about this, and owns up to the possibility that his conclusions might be less than 100% correct.

Now that I am no longer a girl, but a young woman undergoing higher education, I would like to give my own views on the sort of questions I am so often asked, which anyone will be free to quote. First of all, I have to say that I have absolutely no regrets about having been Kumari. Now that I have long got over my initial unhappiness at having left my life at Kumari Che behind, it is wonderful to think back to those times, and it is remarkable that at the time everything seemed so normal. Women came to pray to me for the health of their children, the king came to worship me, people came from all over the world to see me, and huge crowds came out to see me at Indra Jatra, yet it just seemed part of childhood. Looking back, I am proud to have had these unique experiences. Of course I knew very little of the outside world at the time, but that could be said of any number of Nepali children who grow up in isolated mountain villages. At least I had the opportunity to catch up later, so in fact

Somehow I even managed to improve my English. It is still a long way from perfect, but I have more confidence now, and managed an interview for a BBC documentary far more successfully than I had managed with CNN in New York years before.

There were other public appearances as well. Both during my student days and after, as a former Kumari I was invited to be the chief guest at the launchings of several books on the culture of the Kathmandu Valley.[1] Then in 2007, as part of the celebrations for the 250th anniversary of Kumari Rath Jatra (Kumari Chariot Festival), a special ceremony was held at Nasal Chowk in the old Hanuman Dhoka Palace to honour the surviving Royal Kumaris, the first time such a ceremony had ever been held. As I sat on the stage with my seven colleagues, ranging in age from eighteen to over eighty, it struck me how typical a group of Nepali women we were. One was a retired nurse, another a retired pharmacist and four were grandmothers. I was working as an IT Manager, and Amita, who came after me, had passed her SLC and was studying for her Plus 2. The ceremony was well-attended and covered by TV and print media. I gave the keynote speech in Newari. In it I expressed my gratitude to the caretakers who had looked after us as if we were their own daughters and said how happy I was to have been a Kumari and to have spent my childhood representing our culture and country. I also pointed out that Kumari culture is unique to our country and that we should make every effort to preserve the tradition.

My sister Pramila, who had been responsible for so much in our family, finally realised her own dream of of going to the USA on a full scholarship and a teaching fellowship to study for her doctorate in Physics in 2008. With Surmila away working in

---

[1] The three books I launched were: Dr Shaphalya Amatya, *The Religious Dances of Nepal Mandala*; Bhuwanlal Pradhan, *Kathmandu Upatyakaka Kehi Sanskriti Chirka-Mirka*; and Lilabhakta Munankarmi, *Sankshipta Matrika Varnan Tatha Devi Natch*.

Nepalganj, a town on the Indian border, that left me as the oldest sister, but since all my younger siblings were by this time in university or working, I was left with far fewer responsibilities than Pramila had faced.

Pramila, by the way, surprised us all by returning over the Christmas holidays to be married, the first of our generation to "tie the knot". As is always the case when a Newar woman gets married, we all cried our eyes out on the day of the wedding since we were officially losing her to another family. The day after the wedding we, her sisters and brother, were formally introduced to her new husband for the first time and discovered that rather than losing a sister, we were gaining a brother. Soon after the wedding, her new husband returned to the US with her.

Throughout this narrative I have kept harping on certain themes, mostly concerning the mistakes that writers, both foreign and Nepali keep making again and again. I hope I have made it clear by this time that when I was 4 years old, I was not forced to spend a night in a room surrounded by 108 freshly severed goat and buffalo heads in order to prove my courage! Nor did I have to undergo a particularly rigorous physical examination. In fact, if you look at photographs of past Kumaris, it should be pretty obvious that we don't even look much like one another, so obviously we have not have to conform to any mythical physical ideal. If unusually fair skin had really been one of the criteria, I wouldn't have stood a chance.

I am not entirely sure of the origins of these misunderstandings, or if they possibly had a basis in reality in the past, and somewhere along the line became self-perpetuating. As early as 1880, H. Ambrose Oldfield—who had been the British Residency surgeon in Kathmandu for many years—in his *Sketches from Nepal*, told the Kumari story, complete with the little girl alone in the room full of severed heads and her difficulty in getting married. What his sources were he did not say. Were these things that were true at the time, or was he simply misinformed? I wonder if his story was simply accepted as fact and repeated over and over again. Getting at the truth has not been assisted by the traditional secrecy of the Newars about our traditions. It is this secrecy that has led scholars like Michael Allen, whose *Cult of Kumari* is the standard work on the subject, to look to the Patan or Bungamati Kumaris to fill in what they could not learn of the Royal Kumari. Allen is quite open about this, and owns up to the possibility that his conclusions might be less than 100% correct.

Now that I am no longer a girl, but a young woman with a career of my own, I would like to give my own views on the sort of questions I am so often asked, which anyone will be free to quote. First of all, I have to say that I have absolutely no regrets about having been Kumari. Now that I have long got over my initial unhappiness at having left my life at Kumari Che behind, it is wonderful to think back to those times, and it is remarkable that at the time everything seemed so normal. Women came to pray to me for the health of their children, the king came to worship me, people came from all over the world to see me, and huge crowds came out to see me at Indra Jatra, yet it just seemed part of childhood. Looking back, I am proud to have had these unique experiences. Of course I knew very little of the outside world at the time, but that could be said of any number of Nepali children who grow up in isolated mountain villages. At least I had the opportunity to catch up later, so in fact you could say that I have had two lives. And except that I had so much difficulty learning English I cannot see that the experience harmed me in the long run. I have never, either then or now, thought of Kumari Che as a "prison". I still enjoy going back for visits when I am invited at festival times.

Several former Kumaris have declined to allow their daughters to be considered as Kumari. Nani Maya Shakya was quite vehement about this in the *Independent* article mentioned previously, and Chini Sobha Shakya (a distant cousin of ours), who was Kumari in the 1930s, would allow neither her daughters nor her granddaughter to be considered. The obvious question then is, were I to have a daughter, how would I feel about having her considered to be Kumari?

Here I have to agree with my mother. In the 1994 Cosmopolitan article, she was quoted correctly as saying: "If I knew then what I know now, I would never have let her become Kumari." She has, however, modified her views since then because of the new educational arrangements. So along with her, I would say: if I thought a daughter of mine would have to go through exactly what I had gone through, I would definitely say "No". There was so much fuss made over me at the time I was Kumari, but once my time was finished, I was left with nothing but a gold brocade dress and my memories. And more important, I was virtually illiterate.

Yet things have already changed a great deal. The biggest change is of course that a Kumari now has a chance to get some education while she is still serving. In fact, she has excellent private tuition. But there are still other changes that need to be made. For example, serving Kumaris need to be treated a little less like goddesses in daily life. In other words, they need to be less spoiled. It is natural for a child who will not be corrected to order her playmates around and think she is something special, but it would not hurt for a Kumari to be reminded that in a short time, she herself will be a normal child.

My sister Surmila feels that Royal Kumaris should actually go to school like some of the minor Kumaris (as well as Ganesh and Bhairav) do. You can sometimes see them in their red dresses and eye makeup, carrying red backpacks. I actually think this would be going too far, that it would be difficult to arrange and difficult to keep Kumari special if she was riding a school bus every day.

In previous editions of this book I suggested that in recognition of their services to the nation, and the difficult adjustment they have to go through, ex-Kumaris should have a reserved university place or assured scholarship. A big step in this direction has been taken recently: now a portion of the fee tourists pay for their entry tickets to Durbar Square, as well as a small monthly payment from the government, is placed in a bank account to which the serving Kumari will have access when she is 18, assuring that she will have no difficulty in financing her education.[2]

As far as the Kumari tradition now being thought of as a human rights issue, I find this a little confusing. You do not have to look far to see child rights and human rights issues on the streets of Kathmandu. In the mornings tiny children with sacks on their backs go around rooting through the rubbish, others work all day long without any opportunity to go to school. The daily papers give us countless other heartbreaking examples of the plight of the children of our country, some of whom are sold into virtual slavery or trafficked to brothels in India. These are big problems concerning many thousands of children and ones that urgently need to be addressed.

Compared to them, Kumari is only one girl whose only problem is that she is overly pampered. True, she is separated from her family, but she is given another family, and there are no restrictions on her own family visiting. My sisters even used to spend the night when they wanted to. Living in Kumari Che I feel that I was in a far happier position than a child living in a boarding school dormitory. Yet parents continue to send their children to boarding schools, and no one complains of human rights violations. I had a certain amount of difficulty adjusting to the world when my time as Kumari was finished, but that went on for less than a year. I'm sure that my problems then were less than, for example, the difficulties faced by the children of

---

[2] This is for the period while the girl is serving as Kumari. When she goes back to normal life she receives only her pension of 3000 rupees per month.

divorced or separated parents. I have certainly never felt that my human rights were violated.

On the other hand, some positive suggestions have come out of the human rights debate. Child Workers in Nepal (CWIN) President Gauri Pradhan in the earlier *Marie Claire* article is quoted as saying, "Social studies should at least be part of the Kumari's education .... And once out, they need guidance to help them adapt to their drop in status." And in the August, 2004 *Marie Claire* article, a human and women's rights activist was quoted as saying, "She should be given adequate opportunity for development and education, and she should get counselling before she gives up her position." This is not much different from what I have been suggesting.

The point is, that our world is changing. It was only a little over fifty years ago that the Rana oligarchy was overthrown. At that time the vast majority of Nepalis were illiterate. Today things are very different. As mentioned previously, two former Kumaris, Harsha Laxmi Shakya (1955–1961) and her successor, Nani Maya (1961–1969) broke out of the old mould, the former becoming a nurse, the latter passing her SLC and opening a pharmacy. Unfortunately, their example was not followed by the next two Kumaris. When they showed no interest in schoolwork, no one insisted, and it was left first to me, and then to my successor Amita, and our families, to insist on education for serving Kumaris. I think the pendulum has now swung too far in the right direction ever to go back. I had to do all my catching up after leaving office, Amita had to do some catching up after she was finally given tutors a few years into her term. Her succesor was able to continue right from where she left off in kindergarten, and when her time was up in 2008, she was able to go right to her proper year in school.

And of course, there is that question I have always hated so much: is it true that former Kumaris are not free to marry, that their husbands will die an early death? I think it is really time that we put this one to rest. There undoubtedly have been cases in the past where ex-Kumaris' husbands have died within the first year of marriage. But has no one else ever been widowed before their first anniversary? Nepal is one of the poorest countries in the world, and such occurrences are all too common.

Probably the best argument against the marriage legend is Hira Maya Shakya, who was Kumari for a short time in the 1920s. While this book was in progress, she passed away at the age of 88. She was survived by her husband of 92. No problems there. Five of the nine living former Kumaris are married, and are even grandmothers. Of the four unmarried ones, Ameeta and Prity (who stepped down in 2008) are too young, I have been too busy working for my degree and getting started in my career, and my predecessor has never, to my knowledge, shown any interest.

Some of the critics of the Kumari tradition have even called into question whether it should continue. They point to the fact that fewer people are putting their daughters forward. But while this is true, it ignores the obvious fact that Kathmandu families are becoming smaller. A generation or two ago, there were plenty of daughters. As you have seen, I have 4 sisters. A family with 5 daughters is more likely to be willing to give up one to the temporary service of the state than a family with only one or two. It is probably also true that some families have been reluctant to put forth their daughters because of the lack of educational opportunities in the past, a problem that is now being addressed.

I feel it would be a great shame were the Kumari tradition to die. Kumari is a symbol of our nation, as well as a symbol of the lack of enmity between different religions, and I am proud to have been able to serve my country in this manner. As far as I know, Nepal is now the only country where a young girl is worshipped in this way as a goddess. The future of our country at the moment is quite uncertain, but remember that Kumari has remained as a symbol of continuity through two dynasties and the momentous political changes of the 20th century. The more uncertain the times, perhaps the more we need such symbols to keep us from losing our way.

Afterword

In the monsoon month of August 2001, my wife and I made our first return visit to Kathmandu in about 15 years. We had lived there for several years in the 80s with our two young daughters, Maya and Anna Mei (the latter's name had proved unpronounceable to most of our Nepali friends and she was inevitably nicknamed "Laxmi"), then had moved to Japan, and later to England to enable them to complete their educations. Although Nepal was always beckoning, we had somehow never made it back. Then finally, with the children grown up and a university job in Istanbul with very generous vacations, the opportunities to return began to present themselves.

Most of this first trip back was taken up by finding our many old friends and becoming re-acquainted. One person we hoped to look up had been a child at the time, and we had no idea of her real identity. She had been a friend of our two daughters (who had been 9 and 11 at the time we left), but we did not know who she was because at the time we had only known her as "Kumari". Our girls had become fascinated by a child a little younger than they were who lived such a different life from their own, or from most Nepali children. Since we were living in Makhan Tole, only about five minutes away from Kumari Che, they began making daily visits. You have read in the previous pages a little of how their relationship developed.

Young as they were, our girls began to read everything they could find about the Kumari tradition, even forcing their way through most of Michael Allen's anthropological classic *The Cult of Kumari*. Yet even at their age, they could see that much of what was written about Kumari was wrong, and some of it was downright laughable. They urged me to "write a book" about Kumari. It was not a task I felt up to at the time, speaking no Newari and not being sure if I should go poking around in the secrets of Newari society.

More realistically, at every Kumari festival for which we were present, the girls nagged me with requests for photos that would meet their exacting standards. Kumari's two "brothers", Gautam and Mahendra, were very helpful, often allowing me up close to the chariot or palanquin when I would have been shy about barging my way in. The demand to come up with ever better photos made festivals a fairly stressful time for me, but I have always been pleased with the results, some of which are presented in this book.[1]

But to return to 2001. One day my wife was having a piece of jewellery repaired at a small shop near Itumbaha, and we got to chatting with the goldsmith, a member of the Shakya community. It occurred to us that he might know what had become of the girl whom our daughters had known as Kumari, so we showed him some of our old photos of her. "Oh yes, Rashmila," he said immediately. His brother phoned the family, arranged a time for us to go and gave us directions to the house.

We had no idea if she would remember Maya and Laxmi, and did not know what sort of person she might be. After all, we were as subject as anyone else to the tales of spoilt and unapproachable ex-Kumaris. Of course, we needn't have worried. She was waiting in the courtyard for us, thinking that we were probably journalists. The years in Japan, England and Turkey had eroded our Nepali to almost nothing, and we were pleasantly surprised

---

[1] Both Kumari families appreciate gifts of Kumari photos, so anyone who gets good ones during festivals, should make a point of dropping by Kumari Che with 2 copies: 1 for each family.

when she spoke to us in quite competent English. When we showed her the pictures of our daughters, her face lit up and she exclaimed, "Maya-Laxmi!"

After that we were often guests of Rashmila and her family (her mother makes the most wonderful *achar*). She seemed to us to be a normal and self-assured young woman, though she was going through a bad patch at the time: it was not long after she had done poorly on her ISC exam. Gradually, from her and her sisters, we heard the story of how she had gone from pampered goddess to well-adjusted mortal. We also learned from Rashmila herself that she was upset at the number of mistakes both foreign and Nepali journalists made when writing articles about Kumari, and that she hoped to write her own story down someday.

It was on our next visit, during the following monsoon, that I mentioned to them that I had assisted a Japanese traveller and former spy in writing his autobiography.[1] Over the following winter, we agreed by e-mail that I would help her to tell her own story in English.

We began in 2003. By this time she had started her BIT course, and Nepali students are kept extremely busy, so it was only on Saturdays and the occasional evening that we were able to meet. These weekly sessions went on through the monsoon of 2003, we had a couple more during a brief visit in January, 2004, and finished up the following summer. I also spoke with other members of the family, particularly Pramila who was present for most sessions, but also with Surmila, Samjhana, Sunila, Sarbagya and their mother. The whole family was cooperative and helpful, and everyone provided useful insights

You have the results in front of you. These are the memories of a young woman looking back at her childhood. If scholars find them sometimes incomplete, it is because we are now seeing the

---

[1] *Japanese Agent in Tibet* by Hisao Kimura as told to Scott Berry, London, Serindia Publications, 1990.

Kumari world through the eyes of a child, not through the eyes of a trained academic researcher.

Rashmila has had no desire to give away any aspects of the Kumari tradition that she feels should be kept secret. The secrets tend to be rather obscure anyway, such as the mudras used by the priest when doing puja to Kumari, and of little interest to anyone but the people most closely concerned with Kumari. On the other hand, we both hope that this book will clear up the many misunderstandings about the tradition of Kumari, and will also show that with proper guidance and understanding that there is no reason why former Kumaris cannot live normal, happy and satisfying lives.

Postscript to the 2009 Edition: Kumari and the "New Nepal"

Since the first edition of this book, our country has gone through great changes. The civil war that went on for ten years has ended, and the Maoists have joined the political process. This has had a big effect on the Indra Jatra festival, and on the role of Kumari herself.

In 2006, the king presided over the first day of the festival for the last time. On the edges of Durbar Square, the police fought back anti-royalist deomostrators.

2007, the 250th anniversary of the Kumari Rath Jatra (Kumari Chariot Festival), was also the first time there was no king on the first day. The monarchy, though still technically in existence, was suspended, and that year Girija Prasad Koirala who was both Prime Minister and Head of State under the interim constitution, took the king's position at the Gaddi Bhaitak. That year pro-royalist demonstraters were held back by the police, just as anti-royalist demonstrators had been the previous year. The festival seemed to be getting more and more politicised.

Another unusual aspect of the festival in 2007 was that Kumari's carriage broke down before it even got started. It is common enough for the carriage to break down along the way, but for the axle to break right in front of Kumari Che was unprecendented. The prime minister, being elderly, went inside the Gaddi Bhaitak to rest, and so missed the chariot when it finally got going.

On the last day of the festival the prime minister came for his *tika*. Since he was not familiar with the customs, he did not notice that Kumari gave him only a plain red *tika* with her right hand. Then after he left, the suspended king turned up as a private citizen, and was given the large *tika* with rice grains with Kumari's left hand, as was traditional.

It did not do him any good. The following April elections were held for a Constituent Assembly, and the first meeting of the Assembly abolished the monarchy, declaring Nepal a Federal Democratic Republic. Rama Baran Yadav was elected to be the first President and new Head of State. Since the new republic is secular, there is some confusion over Kumari's role and whether a secular state can have a state goddess. On the other hand, shortly after his election, on 22 July, 2008, the new president went to Kumari Che to take Kumari's blessings.

Even though there is some debate about whether the head of a secular state should represent the government on religious occasions, the first day of Indra Jatra of 2008 was attended by President Yadav. Initially, everything seemed to go well, and there was a better spirit than in the previous year. But on the final night of the festival, rumours spread that the government (which had delivered the Republic's first budget that day) had decided to cut off funds for festivals. The chariot pullers went on strike. Ganesh, Bhairab and Kumari, were stranded and did not return home until 3 am. No *tika* was given that night, and the next two days saw rioting all over central Kathmandu. Eventually an agreement was reached between the festival organisers and the government, and the president was scheduled to receive his *tika*, but further rioting spearheaded by Newar groups who claimed they had not been consulted about the agreement, meant that Kumari did not give a *tika* to anyone that year. Unfortunately, politics now seem to have become a regular part of the festival.

Dasain came about a month after Indra Jatra, and with Dasain came a new Kumari. Prity Shakya's time as Kumari from

2001–2008 had seen Nepal go from turmoil to peace, from a kingdom to a republic. She had broken with many Kumari traditions; smiling, laughing and even crying during festivals. She has a lively and outgoing personality which will undoubtedly help her in her adjustment to normal life.

Her young sucessor is now called simply the "Kathmandu Kumari". This time the advent of a new Kumari did not lead to the usual spate of misleading and ill-informed articles in the Western press. Perhaps this is because the Western press already seemed confused over Kumari. In 2007 and 2008 there was a controversy over the Bhaktpur Kumari who was invited to the United States to promote a film made about her. She was usually referred to simply as "Nepal's Living Goddess" without reference to the other Kumaris of the Valley.

On 18 August, 2008, the long-running Supreme Court decision concerning Kumari's human rights was finally made. It said that there should be no restrictions on Kumari's freedom of movement or on her right to attend school. Just what this will mean in practice for the new Kumari is not yet clear.

As to the future of the Kumari tradition and the small girl who has just taken over, all that can be said is that the old days of certainty seem gone forever. As with so much in our country now in early 2009, all we can do is wait and see what will happen.

Special Thanks

In addition to the people already mentioned in the Afterword, a few people scattered around the world deserve special thanks.

In Kathmandu, Kamal Shahi and his family provided exceptional lodgings, with an inspiring view of Suyambunath. Bidur Dangol of Vajra Books and Vajra Publications provided continuous encouragent. In Istanbul, Zeynep Şişman always managed to help me squeeze a few extra days out of the already generous holidays at Istanbul Technical University. Also in Istanbul, Mel Kenne proof-read the entire manuscript and made valuable suggestions. Maya and Anna (Laxmi) Berry also read over the manuscript (in Tokyo, Istanbul and somewhere in the Caribbean), and were our best and most severe critics.